Siqueiros

SIQUEIROS

text by Mario de Micheli

HARRY N. ABRAMS, INC., PUBLISHERS New York

TRANSLATED FROM ITALIAN BY RON STROM

Standard Book Number: 8109-0478-0
Library of Congress Catalogue Card Number: 78-95194
Copyright 1968 in Italy by Fratelli Fabbri Editori, Milan

David Alfaro Siqueiros is not just a painter. He is a polemicist, a theoretician of art, a politician, and a revolutionary. All this must be kept in mind when considering Siqueiros' art. Social conscience, action, and ideology have all worked from inside to form his character and to stamp the expressive qualities of his work. One cannot approach the immense cycles of his mural painting without starting out from the history that has transformed Mexico into a modern nation and from the leading role that Siqueiros has played and continues to play. While it is true that his painting, like the art of Orozco and Rivera, is directly rooted in the Mexican Revolution, it is also true that Siqueiros has succeeded in keeping alive the flame of those stirring days. For he has established an intimate bond with the movement of universal emancipation that is now shaking Latin America from one end to the other. His latest work, the composition known as *March of Humanity in Latin America*, which covers a surface three times as extensive as that of Michelangelo's frescoes in the Sistine Chapel, is evidence of this. The vast multitude surging forward from the walls of a huge octagon is, in fact, the epic depiction of the "Third World" advancing toward its liberation. It is thanks to this vital connection with a movement that somehow represents the continuation of the demands implicit and explicit in the most advanced social aims of the Mexican Revolution that Siqueiros has managed to overcome the crisis of stagnation into which modern mural painting in Mexico has fallen, a crisis brought about by attempts to render mural painting an official and celebrative mode of artistic expression. In short, Siqueiros continued and still continues to nourish, through constant participation in the struggle, the first nucleus of revolutionary inspiration. The revolutionary struggle is so important to him that when he has deemed it necessary he has abandoned painting altogether, fully aware that he would return to it again recharged with new energy and drive.

In studying the various periods of Siqueiros' life, one gets the impression that this artist has lived at least three lives, so filled is his history as man and artist with events, travels, meetings, civil responsibilities, and monumental works. At the age of sixteen he was already conspiring against the dictatorship of Porfirio Díaz, and at eighteen he was in the ranks of the Constitutionalist Army fighting against the forces of the usurping general Victo-

riano Huerta. The young artist soon became a lieutenant and a member of the general staff of the Western Division, which was commanded by Manuel D. Dieguez. In 1925, after the Revolution, he plunged into the work of union organization and led the dramatic mine workers' strikes of the next several years. Finally he was elected Secretary General of the Confederación Sindical Unitaria de México. As a consequence of these activities, Siqueiros was imprisoned, placed under police surveillance, and finally exiled. In 1936 he rushed to Spain, where, as a colonel commanding a brigade, he took part in the bitterest fighting in defense of the Republic. After the Spanish Civil War he returned to the political struggles of the Americas, in Mexico and abroad. He was last arrested in 1960 and spent four years in prison, but was finally released because of the services he had rendered to the nation as an "artist and revolutionary." Throughout all these years he has traveled around the world, driven by his desire to see and to know. He has been in North and South America, Europe, Africa, and Asia. He has given hundreds of lectures, founded and edited newspapers and reviews, established research centers to study the uses of new industrial chemical materials in modern painting, and described and outlined his critical thoughts on art in numerous articles and books. In addition to this extensive and intense activity, he has produced the immense body of painting that the world knows, from easel paintings to the most impressive mural compositions.

All of this, as I said at the outset, must be borne in mind if one wishes fully to understand the Siqueiros "phenomenon," for every one of his acts, and everything that ferments in his soul are closely bound to, and embodied in, his art. One should not make the mistake of thinking that all this varied activity is merely the fruit of boundless vitality. There is no denying, however, that Siqueiros' indomitable spirit and his extraordinary physical power have had a decisive role in the complex history of his life and work. I should say that they have played an enormous part in the way in which he has so avidly mastered certain cardinal ideas of his concept of reality and history. Yet it is only in the conscious relationship between these guiding principles and his boundless energy that his art has found the tension and emotional and intellectual synthesis that distinguish it from the Promethean fatalism of Orozco's work and the pedagogical, circumstantial, narrative painting of Rivera. From this point of view, it seems that the Russian film director Sergei Eisenstein formulated the most accurate judgment. "Siqueiros," he said, "is the best proof that a really great painter has, above all, a social consciousness and an ideological conviction. The greater the conviction, the greater the painter. Siqueiros is not the faithful figural reporter of a great idea created by the proletarian masses, nor is he the ecstatic cry of the individual inflamed by mass enthusiasm. Siqueiros is the splendid synthesis of the conception of the masses and an individually perceived representation of that concept. Between the emotional explosion and the disciplined intellect, Siqueiros strikes a blow with his brush with the implacable certainty of a pneumatic drill on the path leading to the final goal that he always has in sight."

It is not true, as some have argued, that Mexican mural painting is simply the result of an ancient artistic culture that has suddenly reemerged from the past. Siqueiros has always energetically rejected such an interpretation. "Modern Mexican painting," he said, "is the expression of the Mexican Revolution. It is not at all fair to think that this painting is exclusively the consequence of the important pre-Hispanic colonial and cultural subsoil of Mexico, for Guatemala, Honduras, Ecuador, Peru, and Bolivia all share the same cultural subsoil to a greater or lesser degree. Without the Revolution there would have been no Mexican painting." This fact is incontrovertible. One cannot talk of Mexican mural painting without talking about the revolution that freed the country from dictatorship and fostered the reform of feudal economic structures. Indeed, it was by participating in the revolutionary movement that the younger artists began to discover their homeland. Riding and fighting throughout the country in the ranks of the rebel peasants, in the wake of their legendary heroes, the artists learned to know and love their native landscape, their great monumental ruins, and their splendid ancient civilization. The artists learned to penetrate history and above all to feel it live in the hearts of the peons, those simple men with whom their lot was cast. Thus the assimilation of pre-Columbian and colonial culture, or folklore, was not the result of an abstract cultural operation, but the consequence of a creatively fertile, vital process that had set in motion with extreme vehemence a complex of

ideas, feelings, and energies which were decidedly new.

These were the subjects that Siqueiros passionately discussed with other painter friends who had also been soldiers in the revolutionary army when he arrived in Guadalajara in 1917. It was from those discussions, Siqueiros recalled many years later, that "the first theoretical enunciations emerged which were later to form the ideological foundation" of the entire Mexican school of muralist painting. But according to the painter and critic José Guadalupe Zuno, who was present at those meetings, Siqueiros was already vitally interested in all the technical problems of painting and considered traditional painting techniques outmoded. "Even then he talked of painting with a spray gun... of using colored cement." This testimony is particularly valuable, for it reveals one of the basic elements in Siqueiros' creative idiom—not only modernity of artistic vision but modernity in the use of the technical materials most suited for expressing that vision. It is as if one could already hear the refrain that was to return with repeated vigor in his writings years later: "One cannot make a modern art with archaic techniques."

Nevertheless it was not in this sense alone that the idea of the modern attracted his attention in those years. The trip Siqueiros made to Europe in 1919 opened new vistas for him on this subject as well. A look at some of his remarks in the "Tres llamamientos de orientación actual a los pintores y escultores de la nueva generación americana" will suffice to understand how far he had already gone along this path. In these three writings, which are usually referred to under the collective title, "Manifesto to the Artists of America," Siqueiros traced with extraordinary precocity the essential lines of his future creative work, which was to remain open to every new achievement of contemporary artistic vanguards while at the same time it remained aware of the particular problems of the Mexican situation. "Reasonably," Siqueiros wrote in the first "Llamamiento," "we must assimilate all the spiritual unrest of the *Renaissance* that extends from Cézanne to our time: the substantial revitalization of *Impressionism,* the deductive purification of *Cubism* in all its different ramifications, *Futurism,* which provides us with new emotional forces... and the most recent work of *revaluation* of 'classical voices.'" (Dada was still in gestation.) "Let us turn to the ancients," he continued, "for their constructive basis and for their great sincerity, but let us avoid turning to archaic 'motifs,' which would be exotic for us. *Let us live our own marvelous dynamic epoch!* Let us love modern mechanics, which puts us in contact with unhoped for thrills; the immediate aspects of our daily life and the life of our cities in construction; the sober and practical *engineering* of modern buildings stripped of architectural complications (immense bulks of iron and cement planted into the earth); and the comfortable furniture and utensils (artistic material of the first order)."

The influence of Futurist theses in these remarks is extremely evident. Siqueiros came from a country whose economy was still semi-feudal, and he strongly felt the fascination of creative means that put technique, speed, and modernity in general at the center of its interests. On the plane of expressive realization, the intuitions contained in these words of Siqueiros were to remain inert for several years more, but they were intuitions that were to mature in him, grow stronger, and finally become elaborate theoretical convictions that were to be transformed into a method of work and into complex artistic achievements. But if one tries to think of an artist who might be a precursor of Siqueiros, one cannot fail to think of Boccioni and his Cubist-Futurism, at once so impulsive and so firmly controlled, with force lines emanating from objects and people, repeating their rhythm and outlines several times, extending that rhythm to the edges of the picture plane, and releasing bands of structural energies from within those outlines.

In the second "Llamamiento," Siqueiros turned specifically to the question of the need to give the work of art a firm structure. "We draw *silhouettes* in attractive colors, handle modeling with epidermal arabesques, and forget to *conceive* the large primary masses—*cubes, cones, spheres, cylinders, pyramids*—that must be the skeleton of all plastic architecture. Painters must put the *constructive spirit* before the merely decorative spirit. Color and line are expressive elements of the second order. What is *fundamental*, what is the basis of the work of art is the magnificent geometrical *structure* of the *form* together with the conception, interlinking, and architectural materialization of the volumes and the perspective of the volumes, which in their function as 'termini' generate the depth of space. *Create volumes in space.*"

But along with these concerns for modernity and the structure of the pictorial image, Siqueiros nurtured inside himself a desire to recover for contemporary Mexican art the glorious tradition of the past. Actually he received an impetus in this direction from the investigations of the European avant-garde, which had rediscovered African Negro sculpture, the spontaneous expressions of peasant folklore, and the world of the primitives. Although for European avant-garde artists these investigations were part of the general revolt against the styles and conventionality of official art, the problem took on a completely different character for Mexican artists. After all, an African fetish could in the last analysis only remain something alien to a Parisian painter, however much critics and poets might strain to assimilate it into a new perspective of culture. But for a Mexican artist the pre-Columbian past was an immediate and visible reality hovering over him on the heights of the pyramids of Teotihuacán, Oaxaca, and Chichén-Itzá. Siqueiros was totally alive to this fact, that is, to the difference of this problem for Mexican artists. "Let us approach the works of the ancient populations of our valleys, the Indian painters and sculptors (Mayas, Aztecs, Incas, etc.)," he wrote in the second "Llamamiento." "The geographical situation we share with them will permit us to assimilate the constructive vigor of their works, in which there is a clear and fundamental knowledge of nature that can certainly serve us as a point of departure. Let us adopt their energy of synthesis without, however, settling for the lamentable archaeological reconstructions (Nativism, Primitivism, Americanism) which are now so fashionable with us and which are leading us toward ephemeral *stylizations*."

In the third "Llamamiento," Siqueiros lashes out against every form of academicism, even against what he calls "open-air academies," that is, even against those schools which were in opposition to the traditional academy and which in the first decade of this century had attempted a teaching reform and were in some ways influenced by French Impressionism. Siqueiros already felt quite remote from the time when he and his colleagues had organized the famous "pedagogical and political" strike, as he called it, that between 1911 and 1913 had led to the closing of the Academy of San Carlos in Mexico City and to the opening of an open-air school of painting in the village of Santa Anita. Siqueiros had done

Impressionistic drawings from life at Santa Anita, while the drawings he subsequently produced at Guadalajara already began to show a rather dramatic breakdown of his Impressionism. But these were still vague, unconscious, and uncertain attempts, for by about 1918 he had already reverted to a fluid manner that was Romantic in tone. Until the eve of his journey to Europe, his thought and his work both appeared far from being final and certain. His visits to France and Italy in particular were of decisive importance for him. The three "Llamamientos," which he wrote and published in Barcelona in 1921 (in the first and only issue of the review *Vida Americana*, which he founded), were the conclusion of a process of reflection that had been going on for two years, a process that had begun on the day he first arrived in Paris.

It was in Paris that he had been able to examine his own ideas and feelings in the light of the richest and liveliest artistic activity in Europe. It was Diego Rivera who acted as Siqueiros' guide in his first contacts, the Rivera who in 1915 had strained the limits of his Cubist idiom to paint the *Guerillero* (also known as the *Zapatist Landscape*), in which he had expressed his sympathies with the Mexican Revolution in the clearest terms possible. But think for a moment what Paris must have looked like to the young Siqueiros who had just come from a bloody revolution that had exploded in such a cruelly backward feudal country as Mexico. Yet he was not overwhelmed. On the contrary, his exposure to Paris left him more lucid and acute. Needless to say, his reactions were not those of a man without capabilities. There was no figural experience that eluded his eye and no artistic idiom that was not subject to his examination. The fervid avant-garde climate greatly stimulated him, helped to free him of many aesthetic preconceptions, and made him sense new and extraordinary expressive possibilities. But at the same time he realized the incompleteness of certain attempts, the exasperated individualism of others, and the fragmentary quality, the abstractness, and the velleity that threatened even the most serious achievements. How could one make an organic synthesis of all those different experiences? How could one bring them all together in an idiom that could express the thoughts and feelings of a population of poor peasants and workers who, with the Revolution, had suddenly appeared on the stage of history?

These were the questions Siqueiros asked himself. One of the reasons that led him and Rivera to make a trip to Italy was undoubtedly the desire to answer those questions. That is to say, the two young Mexican artists thought that perhaps it was possible to fuse the varied experiences of the avant-garde movements in a unified, broad, powerful, and explicit painting style after the manner of the great Italian painting of the fourteenth to the sixteenth century. The great frescoes of Assisi, Padua, Florence, and Rome had a strong and persuasively evocative effect on both of them. Giotto, Masaccio, and especially Michelangelo must have impressed Siqueiros. Michelangelo's grandiloquent mode of conception and the power and movement of his figures could not have failed to arouse an extremely vivid echoing response in Siqueiros. But it may also be legitimate to suppose that he was not indifferent either to the great Baroque compositions on the vaults and inside the cupolas of the Jesuit churches in Rome. The daring perspective, the dynamic masses, the foreshortening, and the general hyperbolic plastic imagination of these works were made to win the admiration of Siqueiros. In any case, he looked, observed, assimilated, learned, and discussed with Rivera. And Siqueiros also mastered things which at that time he did not think would ever be of use to him. In any case, it was not only the painters of the past that attracted his attention in Italy. Mention has already been made of his interest in the Futurists and in Boccioni in particular, but one should also remark on his attraction to the metaphysical style of De Chirico and Carrà. When passing through Milan in 1919, Siqueiros even paid a visit to Carrà. Siqueiros certainly felt close to this artist's painting, a consistent and solid style without literary frills. If one looks at the *Portrait of W. Kennedy*, a work done in 1920, one realizes that it was chiefly Carrà's metaphysical qualities that influenced Siqueiros. The treatment of space may recall that of the *Builder's Son*, and the mannikin on the left is reminiscent of the *Daughter of the West*. The volume and rigidity of the figure portrayed in the center of the composition are in splendid harmony with Carrà's usual manner of isolating a figure in the center of the canvas to give it relief and monumentality, as in the *Hermaphrodite Idol* and other famous paintings. Siqueiros also undoubtedly had occasion to see some of Sironi's work in Milan. Sironi had just begun to paint the first urban suburbs. In those paintings he charged the metaphysical qualities of De Chirico's *Piazze d'Italia* series with a sense of anarchist and populist unrest.

The Italian and Parisian experiences constituted a period of incalculable value in the artistic and cultural formation of Siqueiros. But in addition to this, albeit on another level, there were the contacts he had, especially in France and Spain, with the leaders and with the most advanced ideas of the European labor movement. In Mexico, Siqueiros had read the texts of Bakunin and Kropotkin and had had some contact with anarchist groups, but in Europe he began his approach to Marxism. Part of his attraction to Marxism can be attributed to the effect of reports from Russia of the great revolutionary changes that were taking place. He was not yet twenty-five years old, and what he had seen and felt in Europe had given him a broader and fuller sense of the problems that the young Mexican painters would have to face at home. They would have to resist any form of nationalistic isolationism in their work and at the same time derive impetus from the energies that their revolution had unleashed. He realized that in this respect he had an advantage over the artists he met in Europe whose works he had come to appreciate, the advantage of being bound with burning immediacy to a movement that was overhauling an entire society. Within that movement, art would have to turn back again to speak directly to men in the name of man. This is what was boiling inside him and what he tried to pour out in the Manifesto he wrote in Barcelona. And this also explains why he could no longer postpone his return to Mexico. The time for study was at an end. Now he had to begin to work.

In describing the history of an artistic movement, one must indicate its antecedents. What were the antecedents of Mexican mural painting? The critics have already described them, sometimes in minute detail, starting from the remotest precursors. Suffice it here to mention the most immediate ones, the ones that provided the direct impulse to the birth of Mexican mural painting. Certainly one of the key figures of the movement was Gerardo Murillo, who used the pseudonym of Dr. Atl. He loved to paint desolate desert landscapes, the desperate and very beautiful land in which the peons were hopeless victims. Siqueiros has written of Dr. Atl that "he was the true political and intellectual precursor of the advanced ideas, ideas that were new from the political and from the aesthetic point of view, and for that very reason he was the theoretician of our movement." Dr. Atl gave concrete form to his thought in 1906, during one of the first major labor strikes in Mexico, the strike of eight thousand miners at Cananea. He published a manifesto in which he argued that in a country without a private art market, public art must be fostered by a new state. While Dr. Atl was the first artist to pose the problems of the new relationship that had to be established between art and the life of the nation, Francisco Goitia was the first painter to depict the tragedy of the Mexican people. This he did in several austere paintings. During the years of the Revolution, Goitia painted the peons themselves in arms and depicted the drama of civil war.

Besides Goitia and Dr. Atl there was a third precursor, the most direct, the most vital, the most popular of them all, José Guadalupe Posada. By the time of his death in 1913, Posada had produced hundreds and hundreds of engravings commenting on every aspect of Mexican life. He did illustrations for songs and stories and, most important, he did *calaveras*, pictures of skeleton figures in which the adventures of living terrestrial beings were depicted in satiric and grotesque humors. Above and beyond his awareness of contemporary problems, Posada's felicitous intuition found an idiom of incredible freedom for itself, a style of spontaneous and natural expressionism. Posada's chief virtue was that he thought like the masses. He was himself "a son of the people." Every picture he produced—full as it was of pungent or good-humored irony and critical sarcasm, bursting with imagination that was truculent and pathetic by turns—had a violent quality that struck out at any form of academic and official art. This is the reason why his work, more than that of anyone else, at least as far as its spirit and the impulse it gave to figural invention were concerned, acted as a vital leavening for the younger generation of Mexican artists who were to give life to the muralist movement.

Siqueiros returned from Europe to Mexico City in September, 1922, and things were already ripe for change. The prospects that opened up before the artists were really exciting, to paint on walls the story of what the Revolution had accomplished in open battle. The aims of the Mexican artists, however, went very far beyond the goals of the democratic revolution itself, for the aims they set themselves were clearly socialist. This is a very special aspect of Mexican mural art. The ideological content of this art for many years represented a rejection of a merely liberal interpretation of the revolutionary break, and the ideological content of Siqueiros' painting still does. In this regard, it is worth quoting from the manifesto that Siqueiros himself drew up, toward the end of 1922, on behalf of the revolutionary Syndicate of Technical Workers, Painters, and Sculptors, a trade union that had just been formed. "Our fundamental aesthetic goal," he wrote, "is to socialize artistic expression.... We repudiate so-called easel painting and all the art of ultra-intellectual circles, because it is aristocratic, and we glorify the expression of monumental art, because it is public property. We proclaim, given the social period of transition between a decrepit and a new order, that the creators of beauty should apply their greatest energies to work of ideological value for the people, so that the final goal of art, which now is an expression of individualistic masturbation, may be that of an art for all, of education, and of battle."

This manifesto, addressed "to native peoples humiliated for so many centuries, to soldiers who have been transformed into butchers by their leaders, to workers and peasants treated with the whip by the rich, and to intellectuals who do not adulate the bourgeoisie," was signed by all the members of the Syndicate, beginning with Diego Rivera, Orozco, Xavier Guerrero, Fermín Revueltas, Amado de la Cueva, Jean Charlot, Roberto Montenegro, Carlos Merida, Alba de la Canal, and Fernando Leal. These artists were the same ones who had put their hands to the first great Mexican mural undertaking, the work done at the Preparatoria, the National Preparatory School, a lay institution founded in the nineteenth century. It was Rivera who had set in motion the new course of figural painting. He started a mural on the subject of the Creation, giving the theme a profane and allegorical interpretation. The others followed after him with the greatest energy.

It was at the National Preparatory School that Siqueiros finally came face to face with the walls he had so long yearned to paint. But he had very little practical experience to fall back on, only a few oil paintings and restless experimentation conducted solely in drawing.

Orozco's experience was far richer. He was thirty-eight years old at the time, thirteen years older than Siqueiros. Richer still was the background of Rivera, who was three years younger than Orozco but had already produced a very large number of paintings. It is no surprise then that the murals Siqueiros painted at the National Preparatory School lack coherence of style and conception. But this is not what counts. What matters, instead, are some tendencies, some means, and a host of initial discoveries, which, together with the resolute plastic energy of some of the images, already anticipate what were to be the qualities and direction of his future painting.

It was not mere chance that Siqueiros did not select one or more flat walls to paint on, as his colleagues did, but chose instead the curving vaults that supported a staircase, together with the walls from which they rose. In this choice one can already see an inclination that he was to develop to the highest degree, an inclination to take advantage of complex and irregular architectural structures in order to avoid the traditional static quality of the frontal visualization point. It is in these irregular spaces, then, that his "first work" was born. The influence of Michelangelo, the Baroque style of perspective tricks, metaphysical synthesism, and archaism are all mixed in Siqueiros' first mural painting. Nevertheless, there are some parts of this painting in which Siqueiros' expressive power already transcends any hybridism of style. And already clear is his peremptory manner of giving voice to an emotion of an aesthetic and ideological nature through the realistic depiction of his characters. Not everything is clear or resolved in this painting, but it is obvious that he had at least framed his questions in an independent manner, a manner different from that of Rivera and of Orozco.

The composition on the ceiling of the first staircase, the one entitled *The Elements*, is certainly extremely experimental in this sense. It is a strong and rhythmic composition of firm geometrical rigor, in which the cosmic symbols of water, fire, air, and earth take on forms that are sometimes figurally recognizable and sometimes mysteriously enigmatic. There are gigantic seashells, solid cones of shadow, cores of flaming substance, and in the center the vigorous figure of a woman borne aloft by a pair of wings. Siqueiros has concentrated the force of the whole composition in this Indian maiden who joins earth and sky in herself. He has subordinated every other part of the composition to her and renounced narrative description in favor of undisputed monumentality. This was a rule to which Siqueiros was to remain faithful even when he painted groups of figures together and conceived gigantic pictures covering exceptionally large surfaces. In his larger compositions, the solution would be to break up the work into several centers of pictorial interest and to establish a dialectical relationship between them, a relationship that would dynamically lead the observer from one to another. But the basic idea of subordinating the descriptive to the monumental was never to be abandoned in Siqueiros' work.

He painted other subjects on the walls of the staircase at the National Preparatory School, but *The Elements* was the most fully achieved and complete, except perhaps for the painting on the right wall of the top landing, the *Burial of a Worker*. Unlike the first murals Siqueiros painted at the Preparatoria which were executed in encaustic, this painting was done in fresco. Siqueiros worked on this painting in 1923, a year after the group of Mexican artists had begun the decoration of the school's walls. The radical change in Siqueiros' subject matter is an indication of what was happening in Mexico at the time. The series of powerful strikes that rocked Mexico in 1922 led to a direct clash with the government. Siqueiros, who was the closest of all the artists to labor and political problems, was profoundly affected by these recent developments. And it was from this situation of struggle that the *Burial of a Worker* was born. Siqueiros did not make use of cosmic symbols in this painting. The subject was one of dramatic immediacy that forced him to the reality of the event without any digressions. But even on this occasion he did not lose himself in episodic narration. The coffin and the workers who carry it on their shoulders form a single block, something compact and solemn. The coffin is in the middle of the picture and looks as if it were hewn, so strongly marked and severe is the foreshortening. The workers' heads are painted in a kind of stonelike relief. A lone woman looks on. She is isolated in space as if to create a sense of centuries of long suffering. There is no lack of symbols in this picture, but the seashells, the dense throbbing flames, and the solid cones of shadow found in *The Elements* have been transmuted here into hammer and sickle. The hammer and sickle are

impressed on the coffin and repeated on a larger scale, like an ideological summation of the scene, on the central wall.

The differences between this fresco and the composition of *The Elements* are not hard to grasp, nor are the points in common hard to find. But aside from the stylistic similarities and differences, like the variance between mass and movement that were to be resolved in Siqueiros' later work, what must be emphasized here is the fact that even in his first exercises the artist already demonstrated that he was a major figure in Mexican mural painting. As for the uncertainties, they were not exclusively Siqueiros'. Rivera's fresco had its weaknesses too, at least in respect to its excessive reliance on fourteenth- and fifteenth-century Italian models. As for Orozco, he felt obliged to destroy some of his murals and paint new ones in their place because he considered them (and in fact they were) too much in the style of Giotto and sometimes too derivative from Botticelli, as in the figures of the angels in *Maternity*. Only in the admirable frescoes of the *Trinity*, composed of a peasant, a worker, and a soldier, and the *Trench* did Orozco succeed in achieving the tragic and austere vehemence that was later to characterize the greatest accomplishments of his artistic imagination. But the *Burial of a Worker* stands up quite well alongside these masterworks, even in the sense of liberation from the religious and even ecclesiastical schemes of figural composition that, in general, had continued to mark the first murals painted at the National Preparatory School.

In any case, Siqueiros could not finish this painting. There were conflicts between the artists and the government, which at this time was opposing and rejecting the more extreme union and political demands. In the end there was a direct clash between the parties. Some artists at the National Preparatory School, instead of choosing the path of celebrative illustration of the Revolution, chose to enter into the heart of the most immediate problems, linking the meaning of the Revolution to the social and ideological conflicts raging in Mexico at the time. This attitude of the artists led Vasconcelos' successor, Puig Casauranc, to take action. Thus, in August, 1924, Siqueiros and Orozco were expelled from the school. Orozco later returned, but Siqueiros never again set foot there.

Fifteen years were to pass before Siqueiros painted

murals in Mexico again. The episode at the National Preparatory School led him to make a radical decision. He turned to political action. He considered this the only consistent way of advancing the most urgent demands of the people that had been released by the revolutionary struggle. His was an uncompromising choice, and Siqueiros certainly paid dearly for it. He was driven away from what was dearest to his heart, mural painting. Thus, while Orozco, Rivera, and others continued the work they had begun on the walls of the National Preparatory School, Siqueiros, always intolerant of any compromise, spent those years leading the most memorable proletarian actions against the government. Many people thought that Siqueiros the union organizer was someone other than Siqueiros the painter, so absolute was the dedication with which the man threw himself into the struggle. Instead of walls to paint on, he found himself looking at other walls, the walls of the prisons of Jalisco, Sinaloa, Chihuahua, and ultimately those of the Federal District Penitentiary. During the time he spent in jail, from May to December, 1930, he could at least pick up his paints again and produce several watercolors and small oil paintings. "Easel painting," Siqueiros called it with obvious irritation, " 'chair painting,' rather, because I didn't have an easel."

He felt he was sacrificing his talent in these small format pictures. But his capacity to conceive an image with a sense of monumentality did not fail him. Canvases such as the *Visit to an Imprisoned Peasant* and the *Arrested Peasant* have a real grandeur in their manner of composition and in the generalized idea of the image. Even in small format, then, Siqueiros never painted the anecdotal, but always described situations and the truth of the human condition in its clash with history. It was this search for truth that inspired his experiments with the development of form, and the line of his development was not to change substantially even when the process of stylistic simplification of this period was succeeded by much richer and more complex expressive invention. At this point, however, his line of development remained that of the *Burial of a Worker*, although there were already signs of the evolution of the first embryonic intuitions that he had had in painting the encaustic mural of *The Elements*. Working obstinately at these problems during the year he spent under police surveillance in

Taxco, he painted a number of pictures that take their place among the most significant works of the period.

These works were painted on canvas, of course, but the format was larger. Some of his canvases were more than six feet in length, and thus he worked with less discomfort. The *Peasant Mother*, the *Proletarian Mother*, *Emiliano Zapata*, and the *Mine Disaster* are among the finest of the hundred or so pictures that Siqueiros painted in that brief period at Taxco, from the end of 1930 till January, 1932. They are unforgettable pictures that make a lasting impression on the mind and on the heart. The crouching figure of the proletarian mother is all but crushed between the walls of a prison, while the peasant mother is tightly framed by two cactus plants in an arid desert landscape. These two pictures are tragic images of Mexico, and in no way are they merely exotic or picturesque. Nor are they pietistic images either. Siqueiros has condensed, in the pictures of these two women, the long history of the whole Mexican people, a people stricken by every kind of adversity, but a people whose indestructible presence fills the time and space of the entire nation. Hector Perez Martinez was the first to point out this aspect of Siqueiros' art. After he had seen these pictures in 1932, he wrote, "Siqueiros paints according to an inner idea, and he is always alert and aware. This particular quality of his can be shown by a comparison. Given a set subject—an Indian, for example—Rivera would paint a man who 'might have suffered,' Orozco would paint a man who 'is suffering,' and Siqueiros, without personalizing, without even symbolizing, but rather, consciously following an inner idea, would paint 'suffering.' "

In the year he was confined to Taxco, Siqueiros had long conversations with Eisenstein who was then taking thousands and thousands of feet of film for what was to have been the motion picture *Que Viva México!* Perhaps insufficient attention has been paid to the conversations Siqueiros had with the great Russian film director. It was a dialogue between two men animated by the same political and social passions and by similar artistic interests. Eisenstein's formulation that "a really great artist has, above all, a great social consciousness and a great ideological conviction" might have been a reference to himself as well as to Siqueiros. This means that he felt a lively affinity for the young and indomitable Mexican painter who wanted to make painting an epic and collective art. Certainly Siqueiros must have explained to Eisenstein particular aspects and significances of the Mexican people and their history and revolution. The dialectical exuberance that still distinguishes Siqueiros' conversation today must also have illuminated the elements of his style, and, more importantly, his conception of a contemporary figural art that would be new in means as well as in conception. But surely Eisenstein told him his views on the possible reciprocal relationships between cinema and art, on the particular qualities of the photographic image and the continuity of film movement, and on the synthesis of cinematic images effected during the process of film cutting and editing. Perhaps there is a trace of the conversations with Eisenstein in the ideas that Siqueiros expressed less than two years later in his argument with Rivera. "The still camera and the motion picture camera for the first time in history offer us... the subtlest and amplest elements of space, of volume in space, of movement in all its complexity, and what is of most importance, the subtlest objective and subjective confirmations of the human drama."

In Taxco, Siqueiros also made friends with the American poet Hart Crane, who in April, 1932, was to end his life tragically by jumping into the waters of the Gulf of Mexico during his voyage back to America. Crane had only recently finished his major poem dedicated to the Brooklyn Bridge. In that poem, which shows some traces of the influence of Walt Whitman, Crane essayed a paean to modern American civilization, without masking those aspects of it which were brutal and inimical to man. Siqueiros was fertile ground for assimilating the visions of a vigorous industrial society that was far ahead of the feudal backwardness that still characterized Mexico. "Down Wall, from girder into street noon leaks, / A rip-tooth of the sky's acetylene; / All afternoon the cloud-flown derricks turn... / Thy cables breathe the North Atlantic still." Such images must have fascinated Siqueiros. This was probably why he settled on the United States as his place of exile when the Mexican government offered him the choice of prison or exile. Recalling this first visit to the United States, Siqueiros confessed many years later: "To complete my experience, which included my activity as a Romantic mural painter, my union and political background in the world of the workers, as well as the activities that sent me to prison, I still had had no contact with a great industrial society. Thanks to a host of professional difficulties and veritable accidents, the highly advanced technology of the United States made me realize that all the materials of our first muralist attempts were archaic and anachronistic."

Rivera was also to say something of the sort. He had gone to the United States a little more than a year earlier. "In Mexico I felt encouraged to go ahead by the warm sympathy of the peasant masses for my work. But I felt that I was still missing some experience really to paint the modern world in all its aspects. What I lacked was the experience of technological civilization, the experience of industrial life. Mexico could not offer me that. Mexico is an agrarian country. This consideration made me accept an invitation to go to San Francisco." What Rivera did not mention was the possible connection between the means of modern industrial technology and their use in mural painting. This was exclusively Siqueiros' concern. It was almost an obsessive *idée fixe* with him. This concern was already evident in the Barcelona Manifesto. Now the question which he had never ceased thinking about returned with even greater force.

When he left Mexico for the United States, Siqueiros already had a goal in mind—Los Angeles, where he had been invited by the Chouinard School of Art to give a course on mural painting. But what better way of illustrating the theory and practice of mural painting than to set out to execute a mural painting together with the students in the course? And that is exactly what Siqueiros did, establishing the group known as the Mural Block of Painters. The outdoor wall on which he was to work was a surface of about twenty by thirty feet. The surface of this patio wall was broken by a door and three windows. Thus there were several problems to be solved. He discussed the project with the architects Neutra and Spolding, who advised him to paint on a white cement base rather than on the usual fresco base. But this decision raised a new problem. Because the cement dried very quickly, the usual technique of traditional fresco painting would be too slow. Thus it was that Siqueiros set aside paint brushes for the first time and turned to the spray gun and to other instruments that were already in common industrial use for varnishing furniture and painting automobiles. Judging by the results, not everything seems to have gone very well, but the ice was broken. It would be interesting if one could look at this first North American work of Siqueiros today, but unfortunately the painting has been scraped off the wall because of its subject matter. Thanks to photographs, however, one can venture some remarks regarding the subject and the execution of this mural.

The subject was that of a workers' meeting on the street. It should be borne in mind that Siqueiros arrived in the United States during the Depression. Factories were shut down, and large masses of workers were unemployed. At the same time a powerful union movement was developing. The theme of his first mural painting in the United States, the *Meeting in the Street*, was dictated to Siqueiros by the reality that confronted him as soon as he arrived in Los Angeles. The compositional solution Siqueiros adopted brings out another of the artist's qualities, one which was already evident in the encaustic painting of *The Elements* but which appears here with greater clarity—namely, the ability to bend architectural structures to his own ends (to the point of integrating them into the composition itself) and to make them just as "expressive" as any other part of the work. For Siqueiros, in fact, a mural painting was never something "applied" to a wall but something incorporated in the very character of the building, forming a unified whole with the architecture.

In the *Meeting in the Street*, Siqueiros has depicted a union organizer with a group of masons and bricklayers. The workmen have stopped the job of building construction or repair to listen to the union man. The building on which they are working is the actual surface on which the mural is painted, a wall with three windows above and a door at ground level. There are workmen looking down from the roof and others leaning over the scaffolding below. At ground level is the union organizer. There are also a father and mother holding their children in their arms. The composition is organized with greater unity than that of the murals painted at the National Preparatory School, and the figures are treated in a manner that resembles a certain twentieth-century European mode, a kind of Cubist-Expressionism like that of Permeke, the Russian Filonov of 1915-18, and the Italian Sironi.

Siqueiros and his collaborators finished the *Meeting*

in the Street in about two weeks. The painting aroused some controversial comments but it attracted genuine interest as well. Another artistic institution, the Plaza Art Center, immediately commissioned a mural to be painted on the façade of its building in Los Angeles. The surface to be covered this time measured approximately one hundred by thirty feet. A different mode of treatment was required because the building stood on a busy street lined with tall buildings, and there were advertising posters all around. As for the subject, *Tropical America*, it was to have been an "innocent" one, at least as far as the commissioners were concerned. A lovely exotic picture with a certain tourist appeal was expected, lush vegetation, birds of brilliant plumage, and female figures in a happy natural setting. Or something of the sort. But what Siqueiros produced was an immense picture of really frightening power. An Indian is shown bound to a cross, while the rapacious eagle of imperialism hovers overhead. This image dominated the center of the painting. To the left and to the right of this scene, pagan idols and the ruins of ancient temples and pyramids, remains of a lost grandeur, were depicted together with rebel peasants emerging from forests of gigantic trees. It was a mural in which archaic monumentality was blended together with popular and Baroque elements, certainly a picture that brought an irresistible visual violence into that dense urban cityscape.

Siqueiros painted *Tropical America* on a dark cement base, using the technique he had already employed for the *Meeting in the Street*. He also made use of a slide projector to transfer his enlarged drawings onto the wall surface. Thus he inaugurated another technical aid that was to be widely employed later. All that has survived of *Tropical America* is the central scene. This is surely the first real example in contemporary painting of what Siqueiros later defined as *pintura mural y esteriora*. Both *Tropical America* and the *Meeting in the Street* represent milestones in Siqueiros' career. When he went to South America shortly after his stay in America, it was these two murals that gave new energy to the ideas he expressed in his writings and lectures. His experience in the United States had given him new courage and new ardor. It had given him a taste of the extraordinary new possibilities open to civic painting. "We will work on the most visible external walls of the large modern buildings, in the most strategic points of workers' neighborhoods, in union headquarters, in public squares, in sports stadiums, and in open-air theaters," he said. This was what he thought, and this was what he was preparing to do.

Before leaving the United States, however, Siqueiros painted one more mural, in Santa Monica, for the film director Dudley Murphy. The *Portrait of Mexico* covers about 170 square feet of wall surface and is divided into three sections. The subject is merely the continuation of the large Los Angeles mural. The center section of this triptych is certainly the best constructed. Two peasants have been slain and left lying on a road. The foreshortening in the foreground is particularly interesting, for it constitutes the first treatment of a formal device that Siqueiros was to employ often. A head and bust are treated in broad and bold terms, but the legs suddenly grow short toward the background, creating a surprising contraction of the space, almost as if the figure were being crushed.

There were more experiments to come before his development would be complete. Siqueiros continued his evolution in Argentina, where the publisher Natalio Botana commissioned him to decorate a bar created out of a half-basement in his country house. Siqueiros liked the room at once because of the difficulties it raised and because of the new possibilities of experimentation it offered him. The room looked like a tunnel, the inside of a cylinder horizontally cut in half. Siqueiros used collaborators in Argentina too, Antonio Berni and Juan C. Castagnino among others. The title of the mural, *Plastic Exercise,* is self-explanatory. An exercise is what it was, for in this painting Siqueiros utilized all the resources of his inventive spirit to discover various applications of the methods he had already tried out in Los Angeles. And he tested other methods that he had thought out already but not yet explored. The pretext of the exercise was to depict a female nude as if it were refracted by a prism in a series of images covering the entire wall surface. The slide projector played a decisive role on this occasion. Again Siqueiros turned to spray painting. This time he applied silicate paints to a dry cement base. This was another one of his innovations in the use of chemical materials in mural painting.

Siqueiros had another opportunity to exercise his inquiring spirit and test the new materials that industry placed at the artist's disposal when, in 1936, he went to New York to establish the Experimental Workshop. In the year he spent in New York with a group of young artists that included Jackson Pollock (who obviously profited most from the experience), Siqueiros explored the properties of pyroxylin and the relationship between painting and photography. In the field of formal and technical experimentation, Siqueiros has always acted with the greatest courage and freedom. And this is why the artist, who may rightly be considered the painter of the greatest social commitment and ideological rigor, is one of the greatest innovators in method, technique, and composition. For example, by the end of 1934 he had already painted several pictures that anticipated Op Art. These were not "abstract" paintings conceived in a geometric style derived from Mondrian, but were pictures based on the study of visual perception and were structured accordingly. And there are intuitions in these paintings that are also related to Gestalt art. But his experimentation in this direction, which was basically schematic, was short-lived.

The year in New York bore other fruits. First of all, Siqueiros approached what was to be known as "matter" painting after World War II. A work like the *Explosion in the City* perfectly suits this description, for pyroxylin is used almost for its own sake as an expressive means. It gives the picture surface a three-dimensional quality. With pyroxylin Siqueiros achieved effects of lumpiness and of heavy and dense corporality that would have been impossible to obtain in oil paints. But this was not Siqueiros' only achievement during this period. He also investigated the "pictorial accident," i.e., those elements of the casual that crop up in the course of an artist's work, those unexpected things that surprisingly emerge from a brush stroke, from a mechanical gesture of the hand, from the hasty erasure that accompanies a change of mind. These accidental elements are often genuinely suggestive to an artist, sparking secret creative processes. It was on these aspects of painting that Siqueiros focused his studies, sometimes giving in to impulse and sometimes experimenting with every kind of unexpected event, consciously setting it up, analyzing it, and later integrating it into a coherent painting procedure. Spots, drippings, and automatic gesture were some of the subjects of his experimentation.

The results of his experiments are clearly evident in the pictures he painted in the year he spent in New York, pictures such as the *Birth of Fascism, Costa Brava,* and *Collective Suicide.* The "material" motif, gesture, and the non-representational element are clearly there, even though Siqueiros uses them in an explicitly meaningful depiction. And the same can be said of his use of the photographic image, which he employed as a direct document of the reality which the artist was to depict and as a genuine aid in forming the composition. Siqueiros checked the casual elements of pictorial accident and the objective elements of the photographic document against his own vision, and although he made extensive use of these elements he never felt that he had to rely on them.

An obvious relationship between photography and painting is evident, for example, in the *Echo of a Scream,* which Siqueiros painted early in 1937. The figure of the crying child is derived directly from a photographic document and has all the objective truth of a photograph as well as its pitiless, analytical impassivity. But Siqueiros' invention goes far beyond this point of departure, strictly faithful as the picture is to the news document, and the result is one of the most dramatic warnings that a modern artist has ever painted. The child's scream spreads among the ruins scattered over a deserted field, and the echo is picked up again and passed on. The impressive force of the image, however, lies in the fact that Siqueiros has painted the echo itself. That is to say, he has reproduced the face of the crying child exactly, but several times enlarged, and this face (just behind the original figure of the crying child) looms over the field and fills the horizon like the image-voice of an imminent tragedy, if not one that has already begun on the other side of the ocean. It is no wonder that this painting, executed in Duco on masonite, makes one think of the method of montage inaugurated and developed in Germany by John Heartfield, for the source of both, photography, is the same.

The subjects of most of the pictures Siqueiros painted in New York (and their titles are an indication of this) are the threat of Fascism, the danger of world conflict, and the tragedy that war would provoke. Aside from the unquestionable artistic merits of these paintings, the lucidity of Siqueiros' political and historical judgment in these works is remarkable. But he could not content himself merely with painting the sanguinary enterprises of Fascism in Europe. Siqueiros' enlistment in the ranks of the Spanish Republican Army was a perfectly logical consequence of his way of living. He was away from America for about two years fighting in Spain. He returned to Mexico in 1939.

That year was of the utmost importance in Siqueiros' life because it was the year he returned to mural painting in Mexico. The more experimental and technical phase of his career was at an end, and the period of his major works was about to begin. He already felt dissatisfied with his earlier paintings and was aware of the rigidity and schematism that had still somehow cramped the full development of his style. This was part of a critical revaluation that he had begun in 1934, the year in which he argued with Rivera. Whatever else one may think of that argument today, there is no doubt that it gave birth to a vast cultural reappraisal which in the end gave new vigor to the muralist movement in Mexico. By the time Siqueiros returned to Mexico, in 1939, both Rivera and Orozco had already painted thousands and thousands of square feet of walls. In 1928 Rivera had finished the 235 frescoes for the Ministry of Public Education Building, the Secretaria, and for the Chapel of the National School of Agriculture in Chapingo. In 1930 he had completed the decoration of the Palacio de Cortes in Cuernavaca, and in 1935 he had painted the first of the murals for the staircase of the National Palace. As for Orozco, he had already finished or was finishing his masterpieces in Guadalajara when Siqueiros returned to Mexico. Many people in Mexico agreed with Rivera when, in the heat of his argument with Siqueiros, he uttered the now famous phrase, "Siqueiros talks, Rivera paints." And, in fact, when compared to the number of frescoes Rivera had painted, Siqueiros' murals could be counted on the fingers of one hand. What is more, no one in Mexico had ever seen them. So expectation and interest ran high when Siqueiros announced his plans for murals in the headquarters of the Electrical Workers' Union.

More than he had been able to do in previous works, Siqueiros conceived and discussed the project with a group of mature artists who shared his political orientation, men like Luis Arenal, Antonio Pujol, and José Renau. Renau, the Spanish painter, produced a number of exemplary works in the field of political photomontage. Two other Spanish artists also took part in the project, though not continuously. They were Antonio Rodriguez Luna and Miguel Prieto, two excellent painters who worked in a style that was realistic and imaginary at the same time that it tended toward the surreal. All these artists had lived through the drama of the Spanish Civil War and shared a painful and vivid memory of the event.

The subject decided upon was the *Trial of Fascism*, but Siqueiros later entitled the work *Portrait of the Bourgeoisie*. It was a burning theme for it forcefully drew attention to the ultimate sources of Naziism and Fascism, causes that were not only European but inherent in the very economic nature of industrial and financial capital. Because of its critical stance, the thesis of the picture was anything but simple. It was necessary to depict both the structures as well as the contradictions of society, and the artist had to expose the most hidden roots of brutality which had already unleashed and which were again preparing to unleash terror and destruction. To resolve these difficulties, Siqueiros had to call upon all his previous experience and reconsider it in the light of his most recent thoughts. Once again, then, he turned to allegory, but allegory free of abstractions, a kind of allegory in which every image would be invested with total concreteness, real weight, and real life impulse. This decision was to become the key to his mural painting. It was ideology itself that was transformed into pictorial image and realistic allegory. And his imagination refused to stop for any obstacle. Siqueiros adopted a method that assaulted the closed spaces of wall surfaces and opened up several new dimensions from which groups of tremendously powerful figures burst forth in violent and deformed depictions.

The differences between the wall paintings of the National Preparatory School and the mural for the Electrical Workers' Union Building had to be profound. Comparing the works of 1922 with the *Portrait of the Bourgeoisie*, one is immediately struck by the extraordinary advances that Siqueiros had made. There is no longer any trace of the hieratic, static quality of the earlier works which were based on an intuitive sense of composition and organized according to an elementary scheme that remained essentially the scheme of frontal perspective, despite the artist's attempts to transcend it. In the *Portrait of the Bourgeoisie* all this has given way to a sense of active composition that makes use of a multiple, changing perspective. In this painting Siqueiros has conceived a dynamic architectural space. He has joined different planes, ceiling and walls, into a continuous surface and superposed forms that were painted from different angles of vision. The manner he adopted in this picture was intended to shake the observer out of his indifference, arouse him, stir his feelings, and provoke his judgment. But no one could say that this mural was merely cerebral. On the contrary, even within a pictorial construction so rigorously calculated in its effects, one can still feel a drive and a passion whose energy and vitality are in no way diminished by the fact that they are controlled stylistically.

But perhaps it is easier today than it was then to grasp the importance and the novelty of this masterful work, which creatively unites the most advanced experiments of contemporary art with a host of moral comments that are still extremely relevant and immediate. In this painting, the interweaving of the imaginary depiction and the photographic document reaches a level of rare efficacy. In this work, a painting style that has the acute and veristic hardness of some of the works of the *Neue Sachlichkeit* is harmonized with the synthetic technique of the political posters popularized during the war in Spain; the procedures of film montage are enriched with the qualities of pictorial simultaneity that typify Boccioni's work; and Renaissance space is broken, amplified, and deformed in intersecting perspectives that vanish in the distance or hover in the foreground, with figures that hurtle from the walls onto the observer. The *Portrait of the Bourgeoisie* is not a large painting. It covers a little more than one thousand square feet of surface spread over three walls and a ceiling and enclosed in the area of two small flights of stairs. Yet in this limited space Siqueiros has managed to create an almost limitless view. And what matters most, he has succeeded in impressing a genuine unity on the heterogeneous modes he has employed. Diversities of treatment are controlled and contrasting qualities are harmonized. Nothing could be farther from the "classicism" of Rivera or from the eruptive expressionism of Orozco, yet nothing could be more exciting and stimulating. The crowded walls have a total force that envelops and encroaches on the observer and grants him not even a moment's respite. At the same time, the composition is smoothly organized around some figurally distinct scenes that are quite explicit in their meaning.

At the top of the center wall looms the imperialist eagle, not the eagle Siqueiros painted above the crucified Indian in *Tropical America* but a metal-plated eagle, the symbol of technologically efficient modern aggression. Below the eagle is a metal machine that produces gold coins while it crushes the victims of violence into the earth. And these victims in turn nourish the productive potency of capitalism and the machines of industry. To the right in the painting are military leaders wearing gas masks. To the left are politicians. Wearing gas masks too, they have been transformed into diplomats of war. In the background are concentration camps, a widow and child, and marching troops.

On the wall to the left, the scene focuses chiefly on the figure of the dictator on a podium. He is standing before a microphone addressing the masses and the Nazi army. This is certainly one of the highlights of the painting, for imagination and critical thought are totally united in an extremely perspicacious image. If one tried to identify all the formal elements that are united in the figure of the dictator, one would have to start with the dynamism of the Futurists and finish with Surrealism. Perhaps there are elements of scenic design from Russian and German political theater in the image as well. The dictator is depicted with the monstrously beaked head of a rapacious bird facing in two directions at once. He shouts and waves his arms. Siqueiros has painted the dictator with three arms in an attempt to suggest frenetic gesticulation. In one hand the dictator is holding a pansy, alluding to demagogical sentimentality; in another hand he holds a flaming torch with which he has set fire to the old temple of the ideals of the bourgeoisie. The words *Liberté, Égalité,* and *Fraternité* are carved on the pediment of this temple. The dictator is not actually a real person. He is a mannikin that is screwed into the podium and worked from below by the same mechanical gears that produce wealth and the arms to defend and increase that wealth.

But in contrast to this power, which generates grief and misery, is the scene on the facing wall. A revolutionary surges forward to the attack. He is shown against a background of foreshortened views of an aircraft car-

rier and a tank. The huge figure of the revolutionary dominates the scene. Above him is the sky painted on the ceiling behind a perspective view of metal towers, smoke stacks, and locomotives. The scene on the ceiling seems to emphasize the certainty of a future time of peaceful labor and active liberty.

This detailed description of the subject is indispensable for an understanding of the ideological commitment expressed in the painting, although I realize that mere description can never convey the effect of the marvelous synthesis that holds all the various elements together. Admittedly, the cascade of gold coins which was painted in Siqueiros' absence is too didactic. But the conception of the whole work makes one think of something out of Brecht. It reminds one of the extremely lucid way in which Brecht dissected the components of social reality to show their inner contradictions and exposed the irrationality and ferocity of the existing system and the barbarities that are often concealed by pure technological order. It is this fundamental approach that gives unity to the *Portrait of the Bourgeoisie,* despite its abundance of motifs and images.

With this work, then, Siqueiros resolutely took his place alongside Orozco and Rivera. And it is from this period on that one can begin to talk of the "big three" of Mexican painting, Orozco, Rivera, and Siqueiros. Despite their differences and disputes, these three artists must be considered together, for between them they have shaped the whole Mexican muralist school.

Siqueiros' next work was not painted in Mexico but in Chile, two years later. Once again, political reasons drove him from his native land. After being in prison for some time, he was granted permission by the government of Chile to be exiled to Chillán, where he was entrusted with the decoration of the Escuela México. The room in which he was to work this time was very large, a rectangular salon the largest side of which was just over eighty feet long. But not all the wall surface was placed at his disposal. The two larger walls were partially or totally occupied by bookshelves, doors, and windows. The two shorter walls and the ceiling of more than two thousand square feet were to be painted. And so he created a mural for these surfaces.

It was a work in which Siqueiros could finally employ his energy with complete ideological and expressive freedom. All the achievements of the *Portrait of the Bourgeoisie* are released in the broad, open, and continuous rhythm of this new painting, and they are sustained by palpitating and powerful execution. One can see that the artist's style had now achieved total independence and the self-assurance of full maturity. And without losing any of his complex and firm rigor, Siqueiros managed to give free rein to all his vivid impulsive nature. Of course Siqueiros painted every inch of wall space at Chillán himself. In this composition he took advantage of the most brilliant color qualities of pyroxylin paint and exploited its substance to create effects of material thickness that give the picture a tactile sense of volume.

In some respects the subject of the work is related to the theme of *Tropical America*, which is to say that he chose a subject connected with the long history of the struggles that the Chilean and Mexican peoples had sustained for centuries to win liberty and independence. Siqueiros has summarized this heroic story in epic fashion in the main characters he portrays. From the earliest hero of legend to the modern leaders of the fight for liberty, their deeds still bear the stamp of immediacy. The history of the Mexican people is depicted on the north wall. In the center of the painting is Cuauhtémoc, the ancient warrior who inspired the resistance against the Spanish Conquistadores. Cuauhtémoc is seen as if from above in a vigorous foreshortened view. The dynamism of his gestures is expressed by multiplying the parts of his body. He is shown ascending the steps of an Aztec pyramid. The bow in his hands still quivers from the arrow the warrior has just shot at the invader lying at his feet. It is this episode that gives the painting its title, *Death to the Invader*. It is clear that with this central figure wearing a crown, Siqueiros hoped to embody an entire people in a single, yet multiple person, an entire people in all the centuries of its history. Likewise, the figure of the man fallen under the blow, and rendered with the same foreshortening as the worker in the Santa Monica mural, embodies all the invaders who have ever set foot on Mexican soil. To Cuauhtémoc's left are Hidalgo, Morelos, Zapata, and the heroine of the Revolution, Adelita. On the right are Càrdenas and Juárez.

Siqueiros painted the heroes of Chilean history on the south wall of the library at Chillán. In the center of the picture is the terrifying, shouting figure of the Aura-canian Indian, Galvarino. With his hands chopped off, the Indian leaps forward impetuously. His head merges into the hairy and bearded head of Bilbao, and farther to the left appears the face of Caupolican. The foreground of the left side of the composition is filled by a complicated play of fists clutching spears, while in the background the figures of Recabarren and Lautaro are framed in a fiery effulgence. On the right, in the middle distance, Bernardo O'Higgins moves forward carrying a banner that incorporates the old and new flags of Chile. Next to him is the face of Balmaceda, painted in unexpectedly subdued colors. The crushed invaders sealed in armor lie at the feet of the heroes in the center of the composition.

The paintings on the two facing walls are not left isolated from each other. The ceiling joining them is brought into action to make a single whole. Broken and torn by lines and geometrical bands, some curved and some rectilinear, the ceiling looks like a blue sky shaken by currents of cosmic energy. Toward the center a kind of vortex of light and fire generates color forms that burst forth, spread out, and descend the south wall to join the movement and colors of the flag, the spear shafts, and the sketchy landscape motifs. The same sort of transition is effected between the ceiling and the north wall. The result is a spectacular achievement that gives new and modern form to Baroque techniques of composition. The constriction and schematic form of the walls is broken to create a free-flowing painted world that is broad and exciting. This is exactly what Siqueiros intended when he spoke of "effecting an authentic transcription of the active, visible, and human world."

After painting three smaller murals in Havana, Cuba, Siqueiros returned to Mexico early in 1944. (All trace of the Havana murals has been lost, but judging by photographs these paintings seem to have been preparations for future works.) It was in a private residence in Mexico that Siqueiros painted his next major work, *Cuauhtémoc Against the Myth*, a picture that covers more than one thousand square feet of wall surface. This painting is almost a continuation of the one in Chillán. On this occasion too, as at the Escuela México in Chillán, he used pyroxylin paint. *Death to the Invader* was painted on masonite, while *Cuauhtémoc Against the Myth* was painted on celotex, but both paintings were mounted on armatures. Siqueiros did not paint directly on the wall because the frequent earthquakes in these regions often cracked the walls. It was not by chance that Siqueiros turned again to the subject of Cuauhtémoc. The story of the ancient Aztec hero who shattered the myth of the invulnerability of Cortes' soldiers provided a neat parallel to that of the presumed invulnerability of the Nazi war machine which the united forces of democracy were defeating on the battlefields of Europe.

Cuauhtémoc Against the Myth has considerably fewer characters than *Death to the Invader*, only three, in fact. On the left side of the picture the centaur-conqueror rears up on his hind legs and brandishes a cross that ends in a knife blade. In the center, in the middle distance, is the timid King Montezuma supplicating the gods. And on the right is Cuauhtémoc preparing to hurl his spear. Siqueiros applies the same technique in depicting the centaur that he used in the depiction of Cuauhtémoc in the Chillán mural. The parts of the body are multiplied. The centaur is a quivering tangle of muscle bands, hooves, and raised arms. Siqueiros has rendered this powerful striking mass more menacing still by catapulting forward the compact play of the multiplied front legs and the large iron horseshoes. The multiplication of limbs in movement reminds us once again of Siqueiros' attraction to Futurist dynamism.

As we have seen, there are some similarities between Siqueiros' style and that of the Futurists, but it is also worth noting that there is a substantial difference between the general Futurist concept of movement and Siqueiros'. There is nothing in Siqueiros to suggest the "cinematographic" quality of the Futurists, just as there is nothing in him of that aesthetic orientation the Futurists derived from Positivism. While the Futurist concept of motion is bound up with a mechanical view of movement, Siqueiros' concept, as one can see from the mural in Chillán and from *Cuauhtémoc Against the Myth*, always involves an ideological meaning. In other words, it is not simply motion that Siqueiros wants to depict but power or overbearing power. Thus he tries to compress the idea of a multitude into the single figure of Cuauhtémoc in *Death to the Invader*, and in *Cuauhtémoc Against the Myth*, all the organized forces of aggression are concentrated in the figure of the centaur-conquistador. In the haranguing dictator of the *Portrait of the Bourgeoisie* instead, the multiplication of arms spinning windmill fashion brings out the paroxysmic hysteria of Fascist propaganda. Thus, although there is in the representation of movement some genuine connection with the early discoveries of the Futurists, one must not overlook the transformation Siqueiros has effected by pressing the purely mechanical representation of movement into the service of the dynamic expression of feeling and ideas. Cuauhtémoc's arm and fist are depicted in the act of throwing a spear, in perfect accord with this interpretation of movement. For the spear itself seems like an organic extension of the hero, and the arm and fist, rather, the arms and fists, suggest the vehement force impelling the weapon as well as the collective wrath that flows into this gesture of insurrection. Thus the epic clash is played out against a background of whirling sky and broad expanses of plains with ancient pyramids in the distance.

The placement of two sculptures at the base of the wall on which *Cuauhtémoc Against the Myth* is painted marks a real innovation. The two statues were sculptured by Luis Arenal after Aztec models, and they were brightly painted by Siqueiros. These sculptures give weight to the two ends of the wall and add a concreteness that balances the upper part of the composition. But these sculptures also reveal Siqueiros' new interest in this form of artistic expression. He was to turn to the medium of sculpture with the low reliefs that were carved in 1952 for the Ciudad Universitaria in Mexico City and again in his largest work, the *March of Humanity in Latin America*, which was finished in 1968.

Siqueiros was to return again to the theme of Cuauhtémoc in 1951. He painted two murals, each more than four hundred square feet, under the collective title of *Cuauhtémoc Reborn*. The individual murals are entitled *Torture* and *Resurrection*. In the second mural, the centaur that reared up menacingly in *Cuauhtémoc Against the Myth* is depicted struck down, lying on his back in the last spasm of his death throes. Cuauhtémoc has donned the Spanish cuirass of the invader as if to symbolize the necessity of taking over the enemy's technology and turning it against him.

For reasons of space and architectural structure, Siqueiros was obliged to adopt a more traditional form of representation in painting the two murals in the Palacio de Bellas Artes in Mexico City. That is to say, he had to use a frontal visualization point. But as usual, even in that restricted space, he succeeded in creating rhythms that break through the limitations and constrictions of the architectural space at his disposal. Perhaps the best example of this is another mural he painted in the Palacio de Bellas Artes, the *New Democracy*. This mural, painted in 1944-45, is enclosed in a low-ceilinged room that offered no possibilities of expansion in any direction. The *New Democracy*, together with the two smaller paintings that flank it, the *Victim of War* and the *Victim of Fascism*, form a kind of triptych. In Siqueiros' *New Democracy*, as in Delacroix's *Liberty Leading the People*, the central figure is a vigorous young woman with bared breast and a Phrygian cap on her head. Her arms are outstretched in a gesture symbolizing struggle and liberation. But Siqueiros' figure of the new democracy is not standing on the barricades. She bursts forth painfully but with irresistible force from a desolate rocky landscape, breaking the lava crust that imprisoned her. On her left lies the body of defeated Naziism, gray as a chunk of cold pumice stone. This figure is depicted with the same kind of foreshortening Siqueiros employed in the figure of the dead worker in the Santa Monica mural and in the figure of the invader in the Chillán painting.

The *New Democracy* is a simple allegory, one of the simplest that Siqueiros has ever painted, but it is an extremely powerful one. The young woman is shown with a forward movement of the arms. A "third arm" comes forward from the middle distance and reaches out into the foreground, parallel to the other two arms. Three hands are thrust out as well. One hand holds a flaming torch, another holds a white and yellow flower, while the third hand is clenched into a furious knotty fist within the flash of a hurricane. Broken chains hang from the wrists of two arms. The symbols and emblems are elementary, but the total image expresses a faith in human, social, and historical values that is eloquently authentic. It is as if Siqueiros intended this painting as a profession of faith in man's historical destiny beyond death and turmoil. And he made no concessions to the wealth of his own inventive capacities in the work. This does not mean that the picture lacks any of the qualities implicit in a singular work of art. Suffice it to say, aside from the total effect of the picture, that there is astonishing artistic

vitality in the details of the painting. Siqueiros must have been carrying this picture inside him for some time, judging by the picture he painted in Havana in 1943, the mural entitled *Dawn of Democracy*.

Immediately after the *New Democracy*, Siqueiros began a new work that was comparable in complexity to the Chillán mural. This was the painting entitled *Patricians and Patricides* that he began in 1945, just after the war in Europe ended. This painting was commissioned by the Ministry of Education. The foundation of the colonial building that was once a customs house and now houses the Ministry of Education, or Secretaria, began to give way. The walls on which Siqueiros was working cracked, and the work had to be interrupted. He was only to return to this project toward the end of 1965, and he was still working on the mural in 1968.

There is another mural painting, begun in 1949, that has also remained unfinished and is still waiting for the time when Siqueiros can complete it. This is a monument to General Ignacio Allende, the hero of Mexican independence. Siqueiros was invited to give a course on the method of mural painting at the Academy of San Miguel de Allende. He still conceived of teaching as a practical and theoretical exercise, as he had in Los Angeles. He selected a room in the former Convent of Santa Rosa, which now houses the academy, and set to work in collaboration with his students. They completed only the first stage of the work. The basic compositional lines were laid out and several zones were painted in solid colors. But this work bore fruit in a book that Siqueiros published in 1951, a book that may well be considered a critical compendium of all his experience in the field of "public art." The book is entitled *Como se pinta un mural* ("How to Paint a Mural"). Siqueiros considers every aspect of the problem, be it technical or ideological, and proposes solutions in the light of his own artistic style. It is a lively book, polemical, and courageous in its ideas and brilliant in its advances. Limitations of space make it impossible to summarize the contents of the book here, but many aspects of Siqueiros' thought on the subject have already been mentioned in the present study. Nevertheless it is worth quoting a few remarks that concern the relationship between the observer and the mural painting, because it is in the development of this dialectically new relationship that Siqueiros was to make further advances.

One aspect of preparatory work for the mural dedicated to Ignacio Allende showing polyangular outlines. The structure of the composition is being worked out, the organization of space is being elaborated, and the various visualization points are being established. (See also the following illustration.)

I have already suggested his position. For Siqueiros, the observer is "a being that moves on a plane and with his own movement activates all the geometrical forms around him." In other words, he is not "the immobile statue of rectilinear perspective," nor is he "the rotating statue of curvilinear perspective." The active observer "so acts that a rectangle is transformed into a truncated pyramid, sometimes tipped to the right and sometimes to the left; he so acts that circumferences become elliptical, and so on." The active observer, then, requires "a new method of dynamic composition and hence a new conception of active space in architecture." In brief, an active observer and a dynamic composition. The methods of traditional perspective and composition are false. For mural painting, "there is only the polyangular method, a method that takes into account ten, fifteen, twenty, and more points of view of the observer in the course of his normal passage over the plane or through the topography of the architecture corresponding to this plane." Thus, this new conception includes the observer within the work of art. It gives him a creative role, because when he moves, he sets the painted images into action, and these images are renewed and changed as the observer's point of visual perception changes. The relationship becomes dialectically dynamic on both sides, because it is a relationship of interdependence.

The mural at San Miguel de Allende was interrupted because of financial difficulties, and the Academy was finally closed down. But what Siqueiros could not finish at San Miguel de Allende he did manage to complete superbly in Mexico City, when in 1952 he was commissioned to paint a vast mural for Hospital No. 1, the "Hospital de la Raza." This time Siqueiros finally found a space waiting for him that was particularly suited to his purpose—a surface of more than three thousand square feet distributed over two walls rising from a semi-ovoid base and broadly curving into the ceiling. The wall facing the mural consists of a large window, while the wall to the right is covered with dark glass.

The subject Siqueiros was to portray in this mural was altogether in harmony with his modern civic conscience, *For the Complete Safety of All Mexicans at Work*. Siqueiros painted it in vinylite on canvas that had been prepared with a nitrocellulose-based plastic substance and transferred to metal armatures. Raquel Tibol, in his exhaustive study of Siqueiros, points out that in this painting the artist had to use an electric sander for modeling, for erasing, and for achieving certain material effects, because of the extraordinary hardness of dried vinylite. But aside from the technical devices that Siqueiros employed, the originality of the mural springs from its total conception. The painting envelops the observer, turns around with him and about him, and transforms the dynamic-constructive experience into an emotional-dynamic experience. Not only does the observer collaborate to give back to the work the entire physiognomy of its structural movement, but he is absorbed by it in turn. Out of this reciprocal relationship is born pathos. Never before had Siqueiros succeeded in making his art live in such an evident and persuasive manner as he did in this painting.

The subject could not be simpler. In the left background is a worker slain by a machine and watched over by his companions. In the center of the picture a procession of women moves forward carrying flowers and grain in a sign of solidarity and trust. On the right, a dense crowd of workers—a miner, doctors, students—march toward a more human and secure future against the background of a billowing Mexican flag. A rainbow arches across a blue, cloudy sky. Above a glowing, fiery red disk appears the figure of a new Prometheus, symbol of revolutionary progress, hurtling down from space. Behind Prometheus, Egyptian and Aztec pyramids, an Oriental pagoda, a skyscraper, and a building out of science fiction, symbolizing the entire history of mankind, tower over the scene. But while the subject is direct and the symbols elementary, the representation, without losing any of its clarity, is conducted with all of Siqueiros' masterly resources. For example, he turns the foreshortening upside down in the flying figure of Prometheus, and produces a series of spatial and perspective changes that make it seem as if the whole sky, with its perspectives of towers and pyramids, were spinning on the ceiling. And the figure of Prometheus seems suddenly to drop and then rise again. To look at this painting is to realize that Siqueiros, as the book on his experience at San Miguel de Allende corroborates, had arrived at a genuine science of large mural composition, a science in which nothing is left to chance, in which everything is calculated, but in which a really volcanic or cosmic talent is throbbing forcefully. This talent is not dissipated in theoretical construction or in concern for content, but vivifies and exalts both theory and subject matter.

Siqueiros' profound natural gift heightens his artistic imagination and allows him to resolve the hardest aesthetic problems without ever falling back on set compositional schemes to be applied on any occasion. When he was commissioned in 1957 to paint a mural for the Hall of the Revolution in the National History Museum, it was this very gift that helped him overcome a host of some of the greatest obstacles he had encountered in his whole career. The subject was one to arouse all his creative faculties, *From Porfirio's Dictatorship to the Revolution,*

but the space allotted to him, some eight hundred fifty square feet on the low walls of a rectangular room, constituted an insuperable restriction. Unable to raise the walls, Siqueiros knocked part of them down. This brought him into an adjoining room, and he was able to spread the mural out over some forty-five hundred square feet of alternately protruding and receding wall surface. In this way he succeeded in achieving horizontally what he could not achieve vertically.

This work was finished in 1967, and it is undoubtedly another of Siqueiros' masterpieces. The visitor enters the double room through a door in a smaller wall on the right side and is suddenly confronted by four "segments" of the story: a tempest-laden landscape, a throng of Cananea miners during the 1906 strike that marked the beginning of the Revolution, a peon on horseback personifying the idea of the populist movement, and a dramatic perspective of dead men, the fallen revolutionaries, laid out on a mountainside. But as soon as the observer steps forward, the central segment expands. The crowd around the flags grows larger, one can see workers carrying a dead comrade on their shoulders, and one can make out, in the complicated play of sombreros, the Texans called in to suppress the rebellion. Moving on to the right, one sees the figures of Porfirio Díaz surrounded by top-hatted ministers, while society ladies dance on the steps of his dais. Around to the left is the tightly knit throng of the people in arms marching toward the observer. As one leaves this room, more figures of Porfirio Díaz's retinue appear and more rebels emerge as well on the shallow walls dividing the two rooms. At the same time the depictions in the first room reappear, but with new plastic values when seen from this new angle. And one sees the figure of the dictator, gray as stone, seated in the middle of a barren landscape.

The various segments of the story merge into one another within a consequentiality that is not merely narrative but specifically figural as well. Other singular aspects of this painting are also worth noting. There are dozens of actual portraits in the painting, not only those of Marx and Bakunin marching together with the workers of Cananea or those of Zapata, Villa, and Obregón with the peasants, or Porfirio Díaz among his ministers. There are also many portraits of humble combatants in the picture, simple men and women, obscure heroes of the Revo-

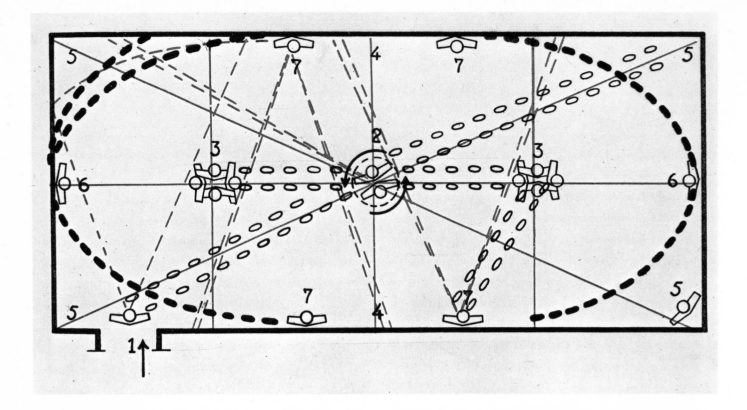

Here is an example of how the principal visualization points of the observer are established. This drawing is the plan for the room in which the *Monument to General Ignacio Allende* was painted (from Siqueiros, *Como se pinta un mural*, 1951). 1: The only entrance to the room; the first visualization point; 2: Exact center of the room; the second and most important visualization point; by turning around on this point, the observer can see the entire painting, including ceiling and walls; 3, 4, 5, 6, and 7: Center of the south half of the room; east and west center of the room: most acute angle of south and north side; frontal view of each section of the work. The path that the observer follows in his normal course over the plane corresponding to the various parts of the architecture indicates the five, ten, fifteen, twenty, or more main viewing points. The transcription of this course onto the architectural space establishes the base of the composition.

lution. Siqueiros did not want to paint a blind, generalized crowd, but a crowd of individuals, a host of real people. And this does not weaken the picture, it does not diminish the energetic drive of the whole composition, for the mural is conceived in a unified and rigorous fashion. It is a work in which the particular timbres of the various colors are released to create new harmonies. The synthesis of form, feeling, and ideology could not be more effective.

This mural marks the end of the period that began with the *Portrait of the Bourgeoisie*, a period very rich in discovery, study, experiment, and results. But Siqueiros never ceases to surprise us. With his huge *March of Humanity in Latin America,* he has initiated a new period of his art, a period in which he is bringing to most impressive fruition his early notions on the fusion of the qualities of painting and sculpture. As I have already said, the first symptoms of this development appeared in the two painted statues set at the base of the mural

Cuauhtémoc Against the Myth. Siqueiros had turned to the problem again in the low reliefs of the Ciudad Universitaria, the compositions known as *The People to the University, the University to the People* and *Velocity*. These concrete low reliefs are covered with mosaic. Siqueiros would have preferred another technique, but financial reasons made it impossible. Finally, with the *March of Humanity* he has taken up the problem again and resolved it. Siqueiros' sculpture-painting is not simply painted metal sculpture. In his workshop in Cuernavaca (the capital of the state of Morelos), where he has executed these works, he has also produced a large number of sculptures painted with special varnishes. But the genuinely new achievement is something else: it is the reciprocal integration of painting and sculpture achieved on panels of asbestos and cement internally reinforced with iron.

Remember that the total surface of the *March of Humanity* is some fifty thousand square feet. For this painting a vast rectangular hall was remodeled and given an octagonal form, but the original proportions between height and width were maintained. At the head of a team of splendid collaborators, Siqueiros painted panels with hundreds of figures. Metal forms in low and high relief large as airplane hangars and are equipped with electric cranes and machines for mixing paints. They constitute a veritable creative factory working on an exceptionally large scale. And the finished product is certainly worthy of the labor that has been lavished on it.

These three views of the same detail from different visualization points show how Siqueiros constructs his images. The slightest movement of the viewing point makes the picture "move" and changes its structure. The detail reproduced shows the figure of Prometheus in the mural *For the Complete Safety of All Mexicans at Work.*

and veritable sculptures in the round have then been applied to the painted surface. These colored metal forms generally repeat the figural motifs already painted on the panels. Sometimes the sculptured elements cover the painted ones, sometimes they do not, and sometimes they add new elements in a dense play of varying volumes and shifting planes, fusing painting and sculpture into a single whole that is unified in rhythm, color, and theme.

This, then, is Siqueiros' sculpture-painting. It has opened up a new era in the history of his career as an artist and in that of the Mexican muralist school. The *March of Humanity* is a gigantic work, and the individual figures are over twenty feet tall. This is the first time that Siqueiros has not had to work in an old architectural setting, and it may be the first time in history that a painter has been able to have a building designed and erected for the purpose of containing a mural painting of this size. I have visited his workshops in Cuernavaca. They are as

Siqueiros wrote, "I conceived the project of a mural painting of such extraordinary dimensions in the close confines of my prison cell. There I painted the two hundred pictures and countless sketches on which this work is based." That was in 1960, when, at the age of sixty-four, he was once more imprisoned for his fiery political opposition to the government. He was released from prison in 1964. The same government that had sent him to prison awarded him, in 1966, when he was seventy years old, its highest official recognition to an artist, the National Art Prize, which had already been presented to Orozco and Rivera. To anyone who asks what is the subject of this last work of his, he replies: "They are crowds, immense crowds setting out from a distant past of misery and oppression and moving forward toward industrialization, emancipation, and progress. It is not only a Mexican theme; it is a theme that concerns all of Latin America."

There are also anticipations of the *March of Humanity* in the two murals that Siqueiros painted in 1958, before his last arrest, the *Apologia of the Future Victory of Medicine over Cancer* and *The Theater in Mexico*. The latter mural is still to be completed. The countless throng surging forward in the *March of Humanity* bears more than one resemblance to the crowd painted in *The Theater in Mexico*, while the monster that leaps out of an apoca-

infuses a blaring note into the immense breadth of vision. What is depicted is the march of oppressed people, but it is an ineluctable march, a victorious march. And above the marching hordes is an adaptation of a motif that Siqueiros used in the Chillán mural. In the center of the ceiling is a kind of cosmic energy source, and from this center—as if from a sun or a gigantic diamond or as if from the luminous eye of matter—waves of energy burst

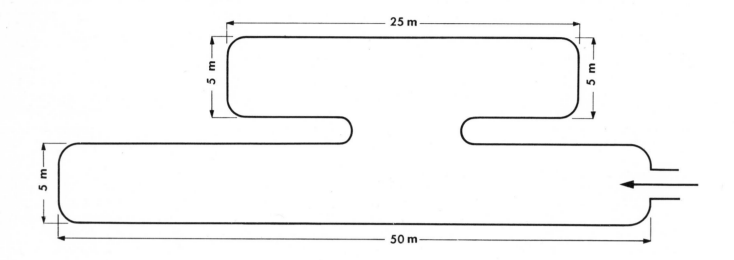

Plan of the mural *From Porfirio's Dictatorship to the Revolution.* The painting covers the wall surface of both rooms. There is a single entrance, indicated by the arrow on the right.

lyptic landscape to attack a woman in the former mural, a monster symbolizing the appalling natural calamities, epidemics, and famines that periodically afflict South America, has a direct parallel in the frightful monster of cancer ravaging living human tissue in the *Apologia of the Future Victory of Medicine over Cancer.* The general conception of the *March of Humanity*, together with its techniques and the invention of sculpture-painting, represents something new and something of which Siqueiros has a precise critical awareness.

Masses of people move along the sides of the octagon in various directions. It is a grand movement that encloses irresistible energy, a movement that is concordant within the diversity of its dynamic impulses. The total effect is one of a relaxed composition, but a composition that is broader in many ways than any of his earlier murals. The sculpture-painting adds an exciting concreteness and tangibility to the total vision, while the violent color

forth in all directions, descending from all sides on the marching throng. But perhaps it would be fairer to say that these billows of energy rise out of the marching crowds and create a new sun of freedom in the heavens above. Thus, the immense room is transformed into a single, continuous rhythm, plastic and poetic at the same time. It is an overpowering rhythm to which the observer gives himself up to become part of it.

The *March of Humanity in Latin America* in the hotel in Parque de la Lama in Mexico City is about to be inaugurated. In these past years, Siqueiros has worked strenuously, up to fourteen hours a day. It seems that he has lost none of the ardor of his youth. I have spoken chiefly of his murals. I should have talked about his easel paintings as well. But in truth, his easel paintings are almost always created in connection with his murals; they are veritable studies for his murals. It is not hard to look at them and recognize the murals to which the paintings are related. And if the mural cannot be identified in the picture, it is a sure sign that it is related to murals that Siqueiros has already started to think of painting in the future. For this is his destiny, what he was born for, to paint man's history on huge walls. In a period in which painting seems to linger in areas of private torment, he emerges as a radically different sort of artist. But there is a reason, and the reason is this. He is the deep voice of the Americas, a voice that has prophetic but not mystical or eschatological accents. The prophesy that emerges from his *March of Humanity in Latin America* is a rational prophesy in which every period of the past and future is given its measure by a historical awareness. And it is in this that one must look for Siqueiros' greatness, for it is this awareness, beyond all other considerations, that gives his work its value and truth.

Mario de Micheli

OUTLINE BIOGRAPHY

David Alfaro Siqueiros was born in the city of Chihuahua on December 29, 1896, the son of Cipriano Alfaro Palomino, a lawyer from Irapuato (Guanajuato), and Teresa Siqueiros Barcenas, the daughter of Felipe Siqueiros, a politician and poet from Chihuahua. David's paternal grandfather, Antonio Alfaro, a native of Michoacán, had fought as a soldier in Juárez's army.

David received his elementary education at the Colegio Franco-Inglés of the Marian Fathers. His studies at the National Preparatory School and the National School of Fine Arts (the Academy of San Carlos) in Mexico City were interrupted in 1913 as a result of General Victoriano Huerta's coup d'état against Francisco Madero.

In 1913 Siqueiros was invited by Dr. Atl to contribute to the paper La Vanguardia, the organ of the Carranzist forces. Then Siqueiros joined the Constitutionalist Army and in 1914 became a member of the general staff of General Manuel D. Dieguez, chief of the Western Division. Siqueiros took part in numerous battles in the states of Jalisco, Guanajuato, Colima, Sinaloa, Sonora, Nayarit, Aguascalientes, and Chihuahua, and reached the rank of Capitano Segundo.

At the end of the Mexican revolutionary war, by express order of Commander-in-Chief Venustiano Carranza, Siqueiros was sent to Europe, with the salary of captain, in order to continue his painting studies. He visited Spain, France, Belgium, and Italy. He made friends with Diego Rivera, and became involved with such post-Cézanne movements as Cubism, Futurism, and Dada. In Barcelona, Spain, in 1921, Siqueiros published the review Vida Americana. The only issue that ever appeared included Siqueiros' "Tres llamamientos de orientación actual a los pintores y escultores de la nueva generación americana" ("Manifesto to the Artists of America"), which was of great importance in the later development of the Mexican school of monumental art.

In 1922 Siqueiros returned to Mexico and, together with José Clemente Orozco, Diego Rivera, Fernando Leal, Fermín Revueltas, and other artists, he frescoed the walls of the Preparatoria, the National Preparatory School. With his colleagues he also organized the Syndicate of Technical Workers, Painters, and Sculptors of Mexico. Together with Xavier Guerrero and Diego Rivera, he directed the Syndicate's newspaper El Machete, which was widely read.

Pressures from the reactionary parties resulted in the interruption of the frescoes at the National Preparatory School, and Siqueiros went to Guadalajara as an assistant to his friend Amado de la Cueva. Cueva died in 1925 and Siqueiros subsequently abandoned painting to dedicate himself to union organization. His work in the labor movement won him the post of Secretary General of the Confederación Sindical Unitaria de México. On May 1, 1930, he was sent to prison for almost a year, and it was in prison that he returned to his painting.

In 1932 Siqueiros went to the United States where he gave a course in mural painting at the Chouinard School of Art in Los Angeles. There began the series of technical innovations in the use of painting materials and instruments and in composition that continue to distinguish his work as an artist.

He returned to Mexico in 1934 and was made President of the National League against Fascism and War. In 1935 he had a serious argument with Diego Rivera. Siqueiros' attack on Rivera constituted the first serious attempt at a critical, and self-critical, revaluation of all that had been achieved in the field of the plastic arts in Mexico after the Revolution.

In 1936 Siqueiros organized the Experimental Workshop in New York, where he investigated the possibilities of "pictorial accident" in painting. His student, Jackson Pollock, was later to develop the accidental possibilities of painting and initiate the school of "action painting."

Late in 1936 Siqueiros went to Spain where he took part in the civil war in the ranks of the People's Army. He was promoted to the rank of lieutenant colonel and made a brigade commander.

He went back to Mexico in 1939, where he founded the review Documental. Together with other veterans of the war in Spain, he organized the Francisco Javier-Mina Society which fostered the struggle against Franco among the democratic forces of Mexico. After a period of fervent artistic activity, Siqueiros took part in the political struggle against Trotsky. The painter was arrested for this, and after his exoneration he left Mexico for the Republic of Chile where he left a permanent mark of his sojourn. The Mexican Diplomatic Mission in Chile commissioned him to paint an important mural in the Escuela México in the city of Chillán.

Then Siqueiros visited Cuba, Peru, Ecuador, Colombia, and Panama, where during the years of the Second World War, he became involved in the anti-fascist activities of the democratic peoples and governments of Latin America. He returned to Mexico in 1944 and resumed his artistic activity. He established the Center of Realist Art with the intention of making new experiments in the fields of painting and graphics. At the same time he wrote extensively on contemporary national and interna-

tional art and published several articles in various papers and reviews in Mexico City. He later collected these pieces in the volume No hay mas ruta que la nuestra *(There Is No Other Road but Ours). In 1948 he gave a course at the School of Fine Arts at San Miguel de Allende which gave him the opportunity to develop many of his ideas concerning the dynamic composition of mural painting in all of its physical and semantic aspects.*

In 1950 Mexico was represented for the first time by its own pavilion at the Venice Biennale. On that occasion Siqueiros was awarded the second prize for non-Italian artists. The first prize was awarded to Matisse. Without abandoning his painting, Siqueiros became one of the guiding spirits of the new phase of development of Mexican art, the phase of "plastic integration," to which he and Diego Rivera made important contributions with works of sculpture-painting in the Ciudad Universitaria, the University City, of Mexico City. In order to provide an authoritative forum for the debate on the subject that was then of primary concern to painters, sculptors, and architects, Siqueiros founded the review Arte Publico. *During this period, while working on other paintings at the same time, he produced one of his most important murals, the one that the Mexican Social Security Administration commissioned him to paint for Hospital No. 1.*

In 1955 Siqueiros visited France, Poland, and the Soviet Union, and in his "Open Letter to Soviet Painters, Sculptors, and Engravers," outlined the position of Mexican realist artists in the face of Soviet and Western formalism. He returned to Mexico and created works that extended and enriched the possibilities of realist art. In 1956 he resumed his travels and visited Europe, Asia,

and Africa. On his return to Mexico he began the mural painting in the Hall of the Revolution in the National History Museum and the mural for the Cancer Hospital of the National Medical Center.

In 1959 he accepted the invitations of the Universities of Caracas and Havana to give a series of lectures in Venezuela and Cuba. When he returned to Mexico in 1960, his efforts on behalf of union and political prisoners which he undertook as president of the aid committee cost him four years of prison, during which time he produced a great number of pictures. At the end of four years he was "pardoned" because of the services he had rendered to the nation as an artist and as a revolutionary. Since his release in 1964 he has continued to work with his usual enthusiasm and energy despite the spinal damage that resulted from his fall from the scaffolding at the National History Museum. Among other works he has completed in these past few years is the largest mural ever painted in the history of art, the March of Humanity in Latin America, *which covers some fifty thousand square feet of continuous wall surface. Siqueiros considers this work the highest achievement of all his experiments and the synthesis of all his discoveries.*

For this enterprise he set up a workshop of monumental proportions. This workshop boasts the most modern equipment and includes a chemical laboratory, painting, sculpture, and engraving departments, and a photographic laboratory. Mexican painters and artists from many countries of Europe and the Americas have worked as a team on this monumental painting, artists who wanted to share the most advanced experiences of a master who, in his early seventies, continues to break new ground.

ONE-MAN SHOWS

Spanish Casino, Mexico City, 1932
Jack Zeitlin Bookstore, Los Angeles, California, 1932
Gallery of the Hotel Ambassador, Los Angeles, California, 1932
Friends of Art Society, Buenos Aires, Argentina, 1933
Delphic Studios, New York, 1934
Pierre Matisse Gallery, New York, 1940
Palacio de Belles Artes, Mexico City, 1947
Gallery of Mexican Art, Mexico City, 1953
Siqueiros' studio, Mexico, 1956
Private museum of Dr. Alvar Carrillo Gil, Mexico City, 1956
Misrachi Gallery, Mexico City, 1964

COLLECTIONS

There is an important collection of Siqueiros' work in the Museum of Modern Art in Mexico City, while the Museum of Modern Art in New York City also possesses a notable body of his work. The largest private collection of Siqueiros' art is that of Dr. Alvar Carrillo Gil in Mexico City. Other notable examples are in museums in São Paulo, Tel Aviv, New Delhi, and Havana. His paintings are in the more important Mexican collections and in collections in North and South America and throughout the world.

GROUP SHOWS

Among the many group shows in which Siqueiros' work has been exhibited, particular mention should be made of the shows assembled by Fernando Gamboa, especially the 1952 exhibit of "Masterpieces of Mexican Art from the Pre-Columbian Epoch until Today." This exhibit, which traveled around the world, had an entire room dedicated to Siqueiros' work. The artist has also been represented in the arts sections of the Mexican pavilions at the Venice Biennale (1950), the Brussels International Exposition (1958), and the New York World's Fair (1964–65).

WRITINGS BY DAVID ALFARO SIQUEIROS

BOOKS

1945   *No hay más ruta que la nuestra*, Secretaría de Educación Pública, Mexico

1950   *El Muralismo de México*, Ediciones Mexicanas, Mexico

1951   *Cómo se pinta un mural*, Ediciones Mexicanas, Mexico
       *Siqueiros: Por la vía de una pintura neorrealista
           o realista social moderna en México*, Instituto Nacional de Bellas Artes, Mexico

1960   *Mi respuesta*, Ediciones de "Arte Público," Mexico

1967   *A un joven pintor mexicano*, Empresas Editoriales, Mexico

ARTICLES, ESSAYS, AND LECTURES

1921   "Tres llamamientos de orientación actual a los pintores y escultores de la nueva generación americana,"
           Vida Americana, Barcelona, no. 1 (also published under the title *Manifiesto de los pintores de
           América*, Madrid, and cited in R. Tibol, *Siqueiros*, Universidad Nacional Autonoma de México,
           1961, pp. 227–29)

1940   "Un ensayo de pintura colectiva," *Romance*, Mexico, vol. 1, no. 4, March 15

1942   "Mi pintura en Chillán," *Hoy*, Mexico, no. 276, June

1943   "En la Guerra, Arte de Guerra! Manifiesto," *Forma*, Santiago, Chile, vol. 1, nos. 8 and 9, January and Febru-
           ary
       "Un hecho artístico embrionariamente transcendental en Chile," *Hoy*, Mexico, February 20
       "La reciente obra mural de Siqueiros en el conjunto del muralismo Mexicano" (written in collaboration
           with Lincoln Kirstein), *Hoy*, Mexico, June 26

1944   "La pintura mexicana moderna," *Hoy*, Mexico, no. 385, July 8
       "La obra de Diego Rivera," *Hoy*, Mexico, no. 387, July 22
       "El joven doctor Atl," *Hoy*, Mexico, no. 396, September 24
       "Carta a Orozco," *Hoy*, Mexico, no. 398, October 7

1948   "Hacia una nueva plástica integral," *Espacios*, Mexico, no. 1, September
       "La crítica del arte como pretexto literario," *México en el Arte*, no. 4, October

1952   "Sobre lo determinante o no de los materiales en cuanto al estilo," *Arte Público*, Mexico, no. 1, December

1953   "La arquitectura a la zaga de la mala pintura" (lecture), Siqueiros' archives, Mexico

1954   "Hacia el realismo en las artes plásticas" (lecture), Siqueiros' archives, Mexico

1956   "Carta abierta a los pintores, escultores y grabadores sovieticos," *Arte Público*, Secundo folleto, Mexico, Jan-
           uary

1966   "Mi doctrina estetica," *México en la Cultura*, Mexico, May 29 and June 5
       "El nuevo realismo mexicano," *Voz Viva de México*, Universidad Nacional Autonoma, Mexico, November
       "El muralismo esta vivo y en marcha," *Politica*, Mexico, November 15

"Vigencia del movimiento plástico mexicano contemporaneo," *Revista de la Universidad de México,* Mexico,
    no. 4, December
"Integración plástica," *Voz Viva de México,* Universidad Nacional Autonoma, Mexico, December

*This list of articles, essays, and lectures by Siqueiros is incomplete. A volume dedicated to Siqueiros'
various texts, from 1921 until now, is to be published soon in Mexico.*

WRITINGS ABOUT DAVID ALFARO SIQUEIROS

1931   Spratling, William, *David Alfaro Siqueiros: Trece grabados en madera,* Taxco, Mexico

1932   "California Group Studies Fresco Technique with Siqueiros," *Art Digest,*
    New York, vol. 6, no. 19, August 1

1934   Edwards, Emily, *Modern Mexican Frescoes, a Guide and Map,* Central News Agency, Mexico
    "White Walls and a Fresco in California," *Arts and Decoration,* New York, vol. 41, no. 2, June

1936   *American Artists Congress,* Two papers presented . . . February 15, 1936 . . . by Orozco
    and Siqueiros, and the catalogue of the exhibition of the Mexican delegates
    . . . at the A. C. A. Gallery, New York

1937   Huerta, Efrain, "David Alfaro Siqueiros: Ducos," *Universidad,* Mexico, vol. 3, no. 18, July

1938   Edelman, Lilly, *Mexican Painters and Their Influence in the United States,* Service Bureau
    for Intercultural Education, New York

1943   Kirstein, Lincoln, "Siqueiros in Chillán," *Magazine of Art,* vol. 36, December

1944   Kirstein, Lincoln, "Siqueiros: Painter and Revolutionary," *Magazine of Art,* vol. 37, January

1947   *45 Autorretratos de Pintores Mexicanos,* Instituto Nacional de Bellas Artes, Mexico, September
    70 Obras Recientes de David Alfaro Siqueiros, intro. by Angélica Arenal,
    Instituto Nacional de Bellas Artes, Mexico, October

1948   Cardoza y Aragón, Luis, "Nuevas notas sobre Alfaro Siqueiros," *México en el arte,* Mexico, no. 4, October
    Fernández, Justino, *Orozco, Rivera y Siqueiros,* Editorial Fischgrund, Mexico

1950   Luna Arroyo, Antonio, *David Alfaro Siqueiros, pintor de Nuestro Tiempo,*
    Editorial Cultura T. G. S. A., Mexico, D. F., November 15

1951   Marcenac, J., "Siqueiros et la peinture," *Les Lettres Françaises,* November 1

1952   Crespo de la Serna, Jorge, "Les circonstances et l'évolution des arts plastiques au Mexique,
    1900–1950," *México en el arte* (special number printed in French), Mexico
    Fernández, Justino, *Arte moderno y contemporáneo de México,* Universidad National de México, Mexico

1954   Cogniat, Raymond, *Histoire de la peinture,* vol. I, Collection Merveilles de l'Art,
    L'Imprimerie André Tournon et Cie., Paris

1955 Cogniat, Raymond, *Histoire de la peinture*, vol. II, Collection Merveilles de l'Art,
  L'Imprimerie André Tournon et Cie., Paris

1956 Myers, Bernard S., *Mexican Painting in Our Time*, Oxford University Press, New York

1958 *Encyclopédie de l'Art International Contemporain*, Prisme des Arts, Éditions d'Art et Industrie, Paris

1959 *David Alfaro Siqueiros*, Biblioteca Popular de Arte Mexicano, Editorial Espartaco, S. A.

1960 Reed, Alma M., *The Mexican Muralists*, Crown Publishers, New York

1961 Fernández, Justino, *Arte mexicano*, Editorial Porrúa, Mexico
  Tibol, Raquel, *Colección de Arte—Siqueiros*, Universidad Nacional Autonoma de México, Dirección
    General de Publicaciones, Mexico

1964 *Memoria del Instituto Nacional de Bellas Artes*, Mexico, INBA, 13, 1958
  Nelchen, M., *El expresionismo en la plástica mexicana de hoy*, Instituto Nacional de Bellas Artes, Mexico
  Siqueiros, Maestros de América series, Dirección de Artes Plástica, Cuaderno 1
  Tibol, Raquel, *Epoca Moderna y Contemporánea, Arte Mexicano*, Editorial Hermes

1965 *Arte/rama Volumen XII—El Arte del Siglo XX*, Editorial Codex, S. A., October 31 D. R.
  Fernández, Justino, *Mexican Art*, Spring Books, Paul Hamlyn Ltd.
  García, Julio Escherer, *La Piel y la Entraña*, Ediciones Era, S. A.
  Gnudi, C., Cassou, J., Ragghianti, C. L., and de Micheli, M., *Arte e Resistenza
    in Europa* (catalogue of the show held at the Museo Civico, Bologna, and at the
    Galleria Civica d'Arte Moderna, Turin), Editori Arti Grafiche Tamari, Bologna
  Gual, Enrique, *Siqueiros*, Galeria de Arte Misrachi, Mexico

1966 Cardoza y Aragón, Luis, *Pintura de Hoy*, Editorial del Fondo de Cultura Economica, Mexico
  Tibol, Raquel, *Siqueiros*, VEB, Verlag der Kunst, Dresden

1967 *Edge*, 5, Fall, 1966 (published in 1967)
  Gual, Enrique, *Pintura Mexicana*, Anáhuac Cía Editorial, S. A.
  La Pintura Mural Mexicana, Fondo de Cultura Economica, Mexico

1968 Rodríguez, A., *La Pintura Mural en México*, Editorial VEB, Verlag der Kunst, Dresden

MURAL PAINTINGS

Myths and *The Elements*, 1922, encaustic (2,150 square feet), National Preparatory School, Mexico City
Burial of a Worker, 1923, fresco, National Preparatory School, Mexico City
Meeting in the Street, 1932, fresco on cement, Chouinard School of Art, Los Angeles, California
Tropical America, 1932, fresco on cement (about 450 square feet), Plaza Art Center, Los Angeles, California
Portrait of Mexico, 1932, (about 170 square feet), Santa Monica, California
Plastic Exercise, 1933, silicon on cement (2,150 square feet), home of Natalio Botana,
  Buenos Aires, Argentina
Portrait of the Bourgeoisie, 1939, pyroxylin on cement (1,000 square feet), Electrical Workers'
  Union Building, Mexico City

Death to the Invader, 1941–42, pyroxylin on masonite and plywood (2,150 square feet),
 Escuela México, Chillán, Chile
Allegory of Racial Equality in Cuba, 1943, pyroxylin on celotex (430 square feet), Havana, Cuba
Dawn of Democracy, 1943, pyroxylin on masonite (80 square feet), Havana, Cuba
Cuauhtémoc Against the Myth, 1944, pyroxylin on celotex and plywood (1,000 square feet),
 Mexico City. (In 1964 this mural was moved to the Union Housing Project in Tlatelco)
New Democracy, 1944–45, pyroxylin on canvas (comprising three panels with a total area
 of 1,000 square feet), Palacio de Bellas Artes, Mexico City
Victim of War and *Victim of Fascism*, 1945, pyroxylin on canvas and masonite, Palacio
 de Bellas Artes, Mexico City
Patricians and Patricides, 1945–68, pyroxylin and acrylic on celotex and masonite (5,000 square feet);
 this mural was interrupted and work is again in progress
Monument to General Ignacio Allende, 1949, pyroxylin on cement base, San Miguel de Allende,
 Guanajuato, Mexico; this mural was interrupted and work is again in progress
Cuauhtémoc Reborn, 1951–61, pyroxylin on masonite (800 square feet), Palacio de Bellas Artes, Mexico City
Man the Master and Not the Slave of Technology, 1952, pyroxylin on aluminum (650 square feet),
 Instituto Politécnico Nacional, Mexico City
For the Complete Safety of All Mexicans at Work, 1952–54, vinylite on a composite of plywood
 and Fiberglas (3,000 square feet), Hospital No. 1 of the Mexican Social Security
 Administration, Mexico City
Velocity, 1953, mosaic relief (240 square feet), Automex Factory, Mexico City
The People to the University, the University to the People, 1952–56, mosaic and low relief (3,000 square feet),
 Administration Building, Ciudad Universitaria, Mexico City
From Porfirio's Dictatorship to the Revolution, 1957–67, acrylic on plywood (about
 4,500 square feet), Hall of the Revolution, National History Museum, Chapultepec Castle, Mexico City
Apologia of the Future Victory of Medicine over Cancer, 1958, acrylic on plywood, National
 Medical Center of the Mexican Social Security Administration, Mexico City
The Theater in Mexico, 1958, acrylic on plywood (600 square feet), Jorge Negrete Theater of the National
 Association of Authors, Mexico City; this work was interrupted and has been resumed again
March of Humanity in Latin America, begun in 1964, asbestos and cement with elements of sculpture-painting
 (50,000 square feet); this mural is being erected in the hotel in Parque de la Lama, Mexico City

COLLABORATORS

Plastic Exercise
 Collaborators: Lino Eneas Spilimbergo, Enrique Lázaro, Juan C. Castagnino, Antonio Berni,
 and the director Léon Klimovsky
Portrait of the Bourgeoisie
 Collaborators: José Renau, Antonio Pujol, Luis Arenal, and, during part of the work,
 Antonio Rodríguez Luna, Miguel Prieto, Roberto Berdecio, and Fanny Rabel
Cuauhtémoc Against the Myth
 Collaborator for the sculptures: Luis Arenal
From Porfirio's Dictatorship to the Revolution
 Collaborators: Mario Orozco Rivera, Sixto Santillán, Roberto Díaz Acosta, E. Batista,
 Guillermo Ceniceros, Electa Arenal
March of Humanity in Latin America
 Collaborators: Mario Orozco Rivera, in charge of painting; Luis Arenal, in charge
 of sculpture-painting; Philippe Stein, Carlo Quatrucci, Artemio Sepulveda, Armando Ortega,
 Guillermo Ceniceros, Adolfo Falcón, Sixto Santillán, Igal Maos, Hedva Megged,
 Marion Bigelow, Carlos Kunte, Raymundo Gonzáles, Guillermo Bravo, Roberto Díaz,
 Estela Ubando, Julio Solórzano, E. Batista P., Enrique Julio Estrada, Fernando Sánchez, and Electa Arenal

ILLUSTRATIONS

In the measurements of the paintings, height precedes width.

32

1 *Self-Portrait.* 1946. Drawing
2 *Nude.* 1931. Lithograph, 15¾ × 21⅝″

WORKS UP TO 1947

3 *The Elements* (detail of the winged woman). 1922. Encaustic. National Preparatory School, Mexico City
4 *Praying Peasant.* 1930. Oil and copal gum on jute (painted in prison). Collection Señora María Asúnsolo, Mexico
5 *Praying Peasant Women.* 1930. Oil and copal gum on jute (painted in prison). Collection Señora María Asúnsolo, Mexico
6 *Peasant Mother.* 1929. Oil on canvas, 88⅝ × 70½″. Museo de Arte Moderno, Mexico City
7 *Mine Disaster.* 1931. Oil on canvas, 48 × 78¾″. Instituto Nacional de Bellas Artes, Mexico City
8 *Proletarian Mother.* 1930. Oil on canvas, 98⅜ × 70⅞″
9 *Portrait of a Dead Girl.* 1931. Oil on canvas, 38⅛ × 28¾″. Collection Señora María Asúnsolo, Mexico
10 *Woman Preparing Tortillas.* 1931. Watercolor. Private collection
11 *Tropical America* (detail of the central figure). 1932. Fresco on cement. Plaza Art Center, Los Angeles
12 *Proletarian Victim.* 1933. Duco on burlap, 81 × 47½″. Museum of Modern Art, New York. Gift of the Estate of George Gershwin
13 *Children Playing at Bull Fighting.* 1931. Oil on canvas. Collection Marte R. Gómez, Mexico
14 *Optical Motif.* 1934. 32¼ × 26⅜″
15 *Explosion in the City.* 1935. Pyroxylin on masonite, 48 × 35½″. Collection Dr. Alvar Carrillo Gil, Mexico City
16 *Echo of a Scream.* 1937. Duco on masonite, 48 × 36″. Museum of Modern Art, New York. Gift of Edward M. M. Warburg
17 *Ethnography.* 1939. Duco on composition board, 48⅛ × 32⅜″. Museum of Modern Art, New York. Abby Aldrich Rockefeller Fund
18 *The Sob.* 1939. Duco on composition board, 48½ × 24¾″. Museum of Modern Art, New York. Given anonymously, 1941
19 *Fire.* 1939. Spray paint on paper, 24⅜ × 20⅛″. Collection Mr. and Mrs. Germain Seligman, New York
   Mural 1939   *Portrait of the Bourgeoisie.* Pyroxylin on cement, 1,000 square feet.
       Electrical Workers' Union Building, Mexico City
20 The revolutionary (detail of the right wall)
21 View of the whole upper part
22 Detail of the ceiling
23 The dictator (detail of the left wall)
24 Detail of the left section of the center wall
25 The metal-plated bird (detail of the central wall)
26 The diplomats (detail extending over part of the central wall and part of the left wall)
27 The military leaders (detail of the right section of the central wall)
28 Study for the mural *Death to the Invader.* Pencil, 44½ × 40½″
   Mural 1941–42   *Death to the Invader.* Pyroxylin on masonite and plywood, 2,150 square feet. Escuela México, Chillán, Chile
29 Overall view of the south wall dedicated to the history of Chile
30 Detail showing the figures of Bilbao and Galvarino
31 Detail showing the heads of Bilbao and Galvarino
32 Detail showing spears and the head of Caupolican
33 Detail of Galvarino
34 Detail of Lautaro and Recabarren
35 Detail of Bernardo O'Higgins
36 Detail of President Balmaceda
37 Overall view of the north wall dedicated to the history of Mexico
38 Detail showing Hidalgo, Morelos, Zapata, and Adelita
39 Detail of Cuauhtémoc
40 Detail of Cuauhtémoc
41 Foreshortened view of the crowned head of Cuauhtémoc

42   Detail showing the stricken invader

43   Detail of the right section with the figures of Cárdenas and Juárez

44   *Allegory of Racial Equality in Cuba* (preparatory sketch for a mural
            now destroyed). 1942. Collection Dr. Alvar Carrillo Gil, Mexico City

      Mural 1944   *Cuauhtémoc Against the Myth.* Pyroxylin on celotex and plywood,
            1,000 square feet. Since 1964 it has been in the Union Housing Project at Tlatelco

45   *The Centaur of the Conquest.* 1946. Lithograph, 29½ × 21¼″

46   Overall view of the mural *Cuauhtémoc Against the Myth*

47   Detail of Cuauhtémoc

48   Detail of the stricken centaur and Montezuma praying

49   Detail showing the centaur's hooves

50   Detail of painted sculpture at the feet of the centaur

51   Preparatory sketch for the triptych of the *New Democracy*

      Triptych 1944–45   *New Democracy.* Pyroxylin on canvas (the total surface of the three
            panels is 1,000 square feet). Palacio de Bellas Artes, Mexico City

52   *Victim of War* (left section)

53   *New Democracy* (overall view of the central section)

54   *New Democracy* (detail of the head of democracy)

55   *New Democracy* (detail of Naziism defeated, beneath the fist of democracy)

56   *Victim of Fascism* (detail)

57   *Victim of Fascism* (detail)

58   Study for the *Guardian of Peace.* 1947. Pyroxylin, 19⅝ × 17⅜″

WORKS UP TO 1968

59   *The Torrent.* 1944. Pyroxylin, 31⅛ × 24″

60   *El Coronelazo (Self-Portrait).* 1945. Pyroxylin, 39⅜ × 48″. Instituto Nacional de Bellas Artes, Mexico City

61   *The Face of Treason.* 1947. Pyroxylin, 31⅞ × 36¼″

62   *Rotation.* Pyroxylin on bakelite, 33⅛ × 28¾″

63   *The Devil in Church.* 1947. Pyroxylin on masonite, 86¼ × 61⅜″. Instituto Nacional de Bellas Artes, Mexico City

64   *Gourds.* 1946. Pyroxylin on masonite, 35⅜ × 47½″. Collection Dr. Alvar Carrillo Gil, Mexico City

65   *Portrait of Orozco.* 1947. Pyroxylin on masonite, 48 × 39⅜″. Collection Dr. Alvar Carrillo Gil, Mexico City

66   *Intertropics.* 1946. Pyroxylin on masonite, 35⅞ × 47¼″. Collection Dr. Alvar Carrillo Gil, Mexico City

67   *Head of Cuauhtémoc.* 1947. Pyroxylin on masonite. Collection Dr. Alvar Carillo Gil, Mexico City

68   *Cain in the United States.* 1947. Pyroxylin, 29⅞ × 36⅝″. Collection Eduardo Bustamante, Mexico

69   *Our Present Image.* 1945. Lithograph, 11¾ × 9⅞″

70   *Our Present Image.* 1947. Pyroxylin on masonite, 86⅝ × 67¾″. Instituto Nacional de Bellas Artes, Mexico City

71   *Rotation.* 1948. Pyroxylin on paper, 24¾ × 29⅞″. Collection Dr. MacKinley Helm, Brookline, Massachusetts

72   *Portrait of Angelica.* 1947. Pyroxylin on masonite, 86¼ × 61⅜″.
            Collection Angelica Arenal de Siqueiros

73   *Death and Burial of Cain.* 1947. Pyroxylin on masonite, 30¼ × 36⅝″. Collection Dr. Alvar Carrillo Gil, Mexico City

74   *Image of Mexico.* 1947. Pyroxylin on composition board, 20½ × 28″. Private collection, Mexico City

75   *The Pyramid of Chichén-Itzá in Flames.* 1948. Pyroxylin on masonite, 35⅞ × 28¾″. Collection Dr. Alvar Carrillo Gil,
            Mexico City

76   *Child with a Mask.* 1949. Pyroxylin on composition board, 48 × 39⅜″. Private collection, Mexico City

77   *Atomic Airship.* 1956. Acrylic. Collection Dr. Alvar Carrillo Gil, Mexico City

78   *Fish Heads.* 1955. Acrylic, 39⅜ × 47⅛″. Private collection

79   *Excommunication and Death Sentence of Miguel Hidalgo.* 1953. Pyroxylin. Collection Universidad de Morelia, Mexico

80   *Don Benito Juárez.* 1956. Pyroxylin, 27⅝ × 19⅝″. Private collection

81   *Landscape.* 1956. Pyroxylin, on masonite, 41 × 38⅝″

      Mural 1951   *Cuauhtémoc Reborn: Torture.* Pyroxylin on masonite, 400 square feet. Palacio de Bellas Artes, Mexico City

82   Sketch for the *Torture of Cuauhtémoc.* 1950. Collection Dr. Alvar Carrillo Gil, Mexico City

83   Study for the *Torture of Cuauhtémoc.* 1950. Pencil. Collection Dr. Alvar Carrillo Gil, Mexico City

84   *Snarling Dog.* 1945. Lithograph

34

85 *The Torture of Cuauhtémoc.* 1950

86 Detail of the appeal to liberty

87 Detail of the mutilated child

88 Detail of the torture fire

89 Detail showing the Conquistadors

90 Detail of Tacuba

91 Oblique view of the *Torture of Cuauhtémoc*

92 Detail showing Malince and soldiers

93 Study for the mural *Cuauhtémoc Reborn: Resurrection*

Mural 1961 *Cuauhtémoc Reborn: Resurrection.* Pyroxylin on masonite, 400 square feet.
        Palacio de Bellas Artes, Mexico City

94 Overall view of *Cuauhtémoc Reborn: Resurrection*

95 Study for the mural *Patricians and Patricides*

Mural 1945–68 *Patricians and Patricides.* Pyroxylin and acrylic on celotex and masonite, 5,000 square feet.
        Ministry of Education, formerly San Domingo Customs House. Work on the mural
        was suspended when the foundations of the colonial building began to give way. Siqueiros
        resumed work on this mural in 1965 and has enlarged the surface of the painting.

96 Study for the mural *Patricians and Patricides.* 1947

97 Detail of the patricides

98 Detail of the patricides

99 *Velocity.* 1953. Mosaic, 240 square feet. Automex Factory, Mexico City

Mural 1952–56 *The People to the University, the University to the People.*
        Low relief and mosaic, 3,000 square feet. University Administration Building, Mexico City

100 Oblique overall view

101 Oblique overall view

102 Oblique overall view

103 Oblique overall view

104 Plan and perspective drawing for the mural *For the Complete Safety of All Mexicans at Work*

Mural 1952–54 *For the Complete Safety of All Mexicans at Work.* Vinylite on plywood and Fiberglas composite,
        3,000 square feet. Social Security Administration Hospital No. 1, Mexico City

105 Detail of Prometheus

106 *Study of Clouds.* 1949

107 Detail above the figure of Prometheus showing the monumental structures of various
        civilizations from antiquity to modern times; the rainbow and the red star

108 Detail showing Prometheus

109 Detail of the right section of the mural with workers and technicians joining forces for national liberation

110 Detail of the central section with the procession of women

111 Overall view of *For the Complete Safety of All Mexicans at Work*

112 Detail to the left of the central section with victim of capitalist industrialization

113 Detail to the left of the central section with workmen standing beside the victim

114 Detail of the victim

115 Study for Prometheus

Mural 1958 *Apologia of the Future Victory of Medicine over Cancer.* Acrylic
        on plywood. National Medical Center, Mexico City

116 Overall view of the mural *Apologia of the Future Victory of Medicine over Cancer*

117 Detail of prehistory

118 Detail of primitive man

119 Detail showing technology in the service of medicine

120 Detail of the monster of cancer

121 *Landscape.* 1956. Pyroxylin on masonite

122 *Erosion.* 1954. Pyroxylin, $35\frac{3}{8} \times 47\frac{1}{2}''$

123 *Foundry.* 1956. Acrylic

Mural 1958 *The Theater in Mexico* (unfinished). Acrylic on plywood, 600 square feet.
        Jorge Negrete Theater of the National Association of Authors, Mexico City

124 Overall view

125 Oblique overall view

126 Detail showing the stage

127 Detail of repression

128 Detail of rebellion

129 Detail of rebellion

130 Detail showing the fallen worker

131 Study for the slain worker in the mural *From Porfirio's Dictatorship to the Revolution*. 1958
Mural 1957–67 *From Porfirio's Dictatorship to the Revolution*. Acrylic on plywood, about
4,500 square feet. Revolution Hall, National History Museum, Chapultepec Castle, Mexico City

132 Detail of the first room showing the revolution

133 Section of the left part of the mural in the first room showing civil war and its victims

134 Detail of revolutionaries fallen in the struggle

135 Detail of the second room, right wall, showing Porfirio Díaz with his ministers and the ladies of his "court"

136 View of the two rooms from the entrance

137 Study for the mural *From Porfirio's Dictatorship to the Revolution*. National
History Museum, Plumon. Collection Marte R. Gómez

138 Detail of the left wall in the second room showing the revolutionaries

139 Detail with the revolutionaries

140 Frontal view in the second room depicting the Cananea strike

141 Detail of the ideologues of the revolution

142 Detail of the fallen worker

143 Study for the mural *March of Humanity in Latin America*. 1963
Mural 1964–68 *March of Humanity in Latin America*. Asbestos and cement, with elements
of sculpture-painting, 50,000 square feet. To be placed in the
hotel being built in Parque de la Lama, Mexico City

144 Sketch for *March of Humanity*. 1963

145 Sketch for *March of Humanity*. 1963

146 Model of *March of Humanity*. 1963

147 Model of *March of Humanity*. 1963

148 Oblique partial view of panels for *March of Humanity*

149 Detail of a panel in progress

150 Detail of sculpture-paintings for *March of Humanity* in Siqueiros' studio

151 Detail of work in progress

152 Sculpture-painting

153 Sculpture-painting in progress in outdoor studio

154 Sculpture-painting in progress in outdoor studio

155 Sculpture-painting in progress, showing a landscape with monster

156 Detail of sculpture-painting

157 Detail of sculpture-painting

158 Sculpture-painting in progress

159 Sculpture-painting in progress

160 Several sculpture-paintings in the outdoor studio

161 Several sculpture-paintings in the outdoor studio

162 Siqueiros at work

163 Siqueiros at work

WORKS UP TO 1947

3

4

8

13

15

16

18

Portrait of the Bourgeoisie

mural 1939: *(1,000 square feet)*

22

24

25

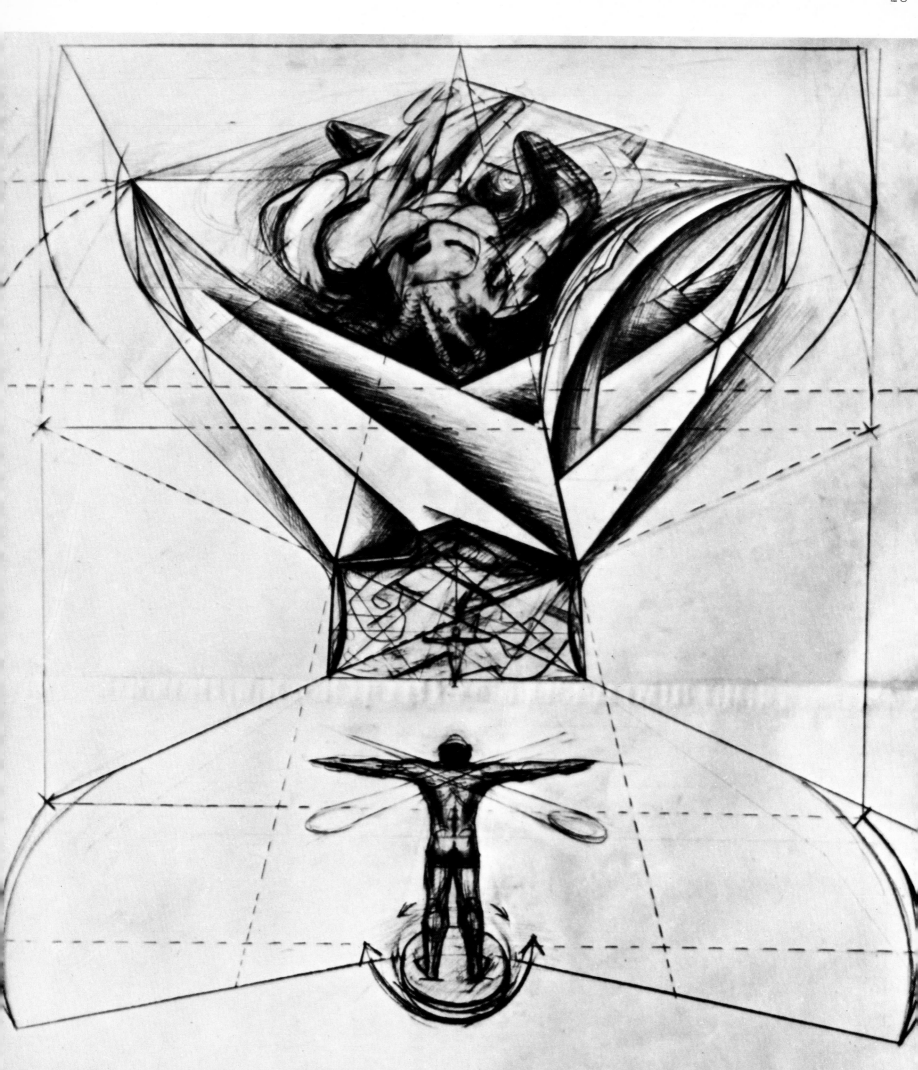

Death to the Invader

mural 1941–42: *(2,150 square feet)*

32

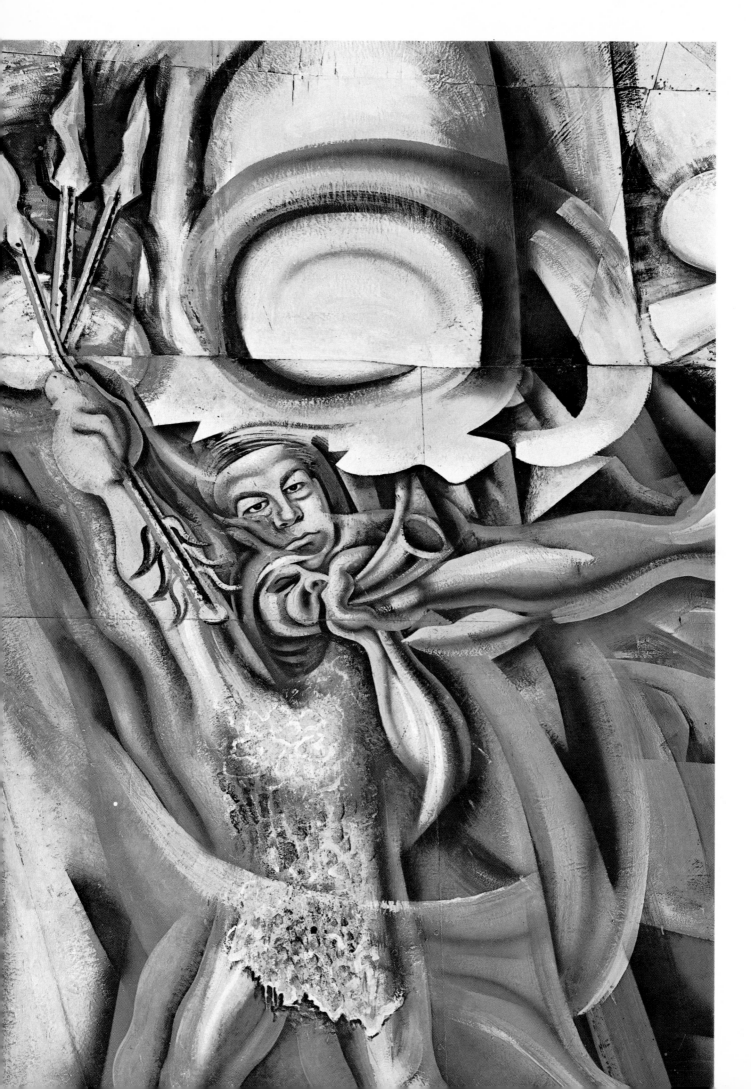

34

36

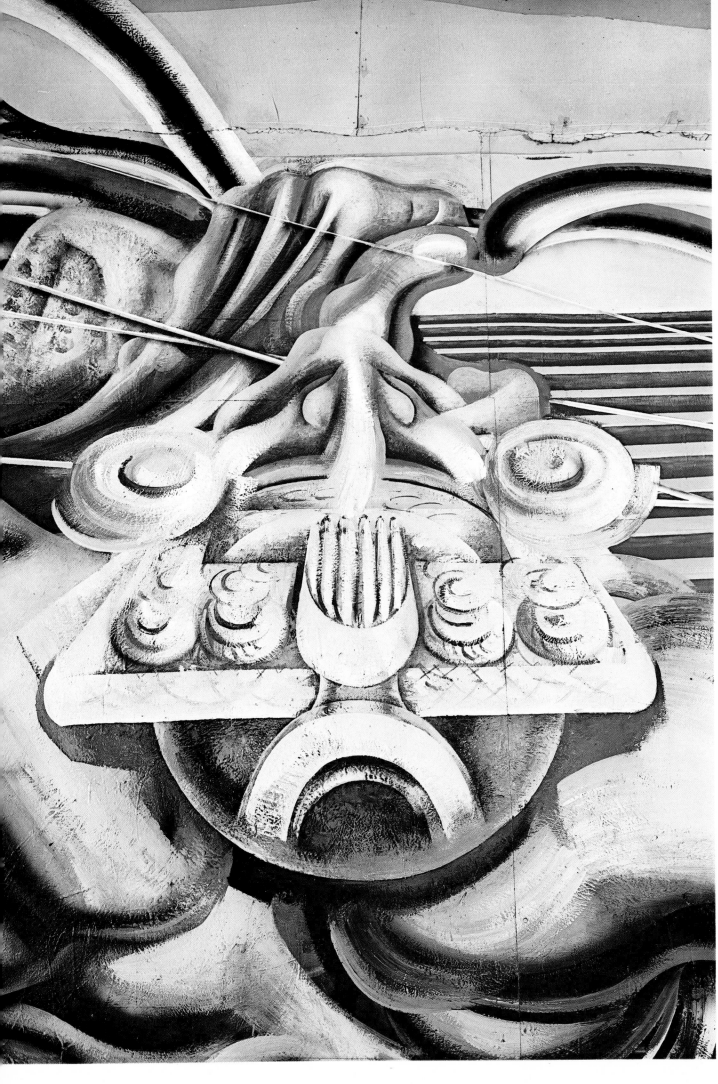

43

Cuauhtémoc Against the Myth

mural 1944:   (1,000 square feet)

47   48

49

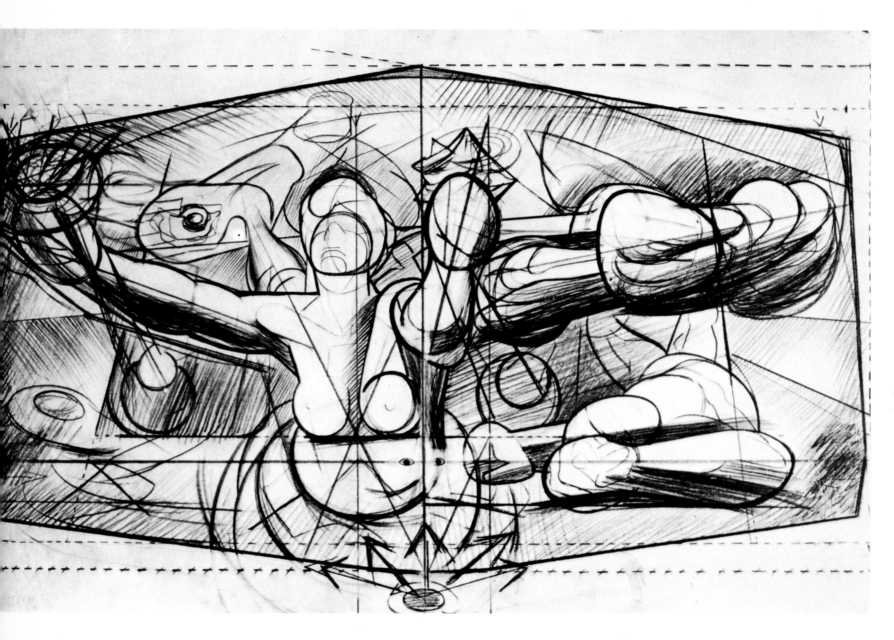

51

New Democracy

triptych 1944–45: *(1,000 square feet)*

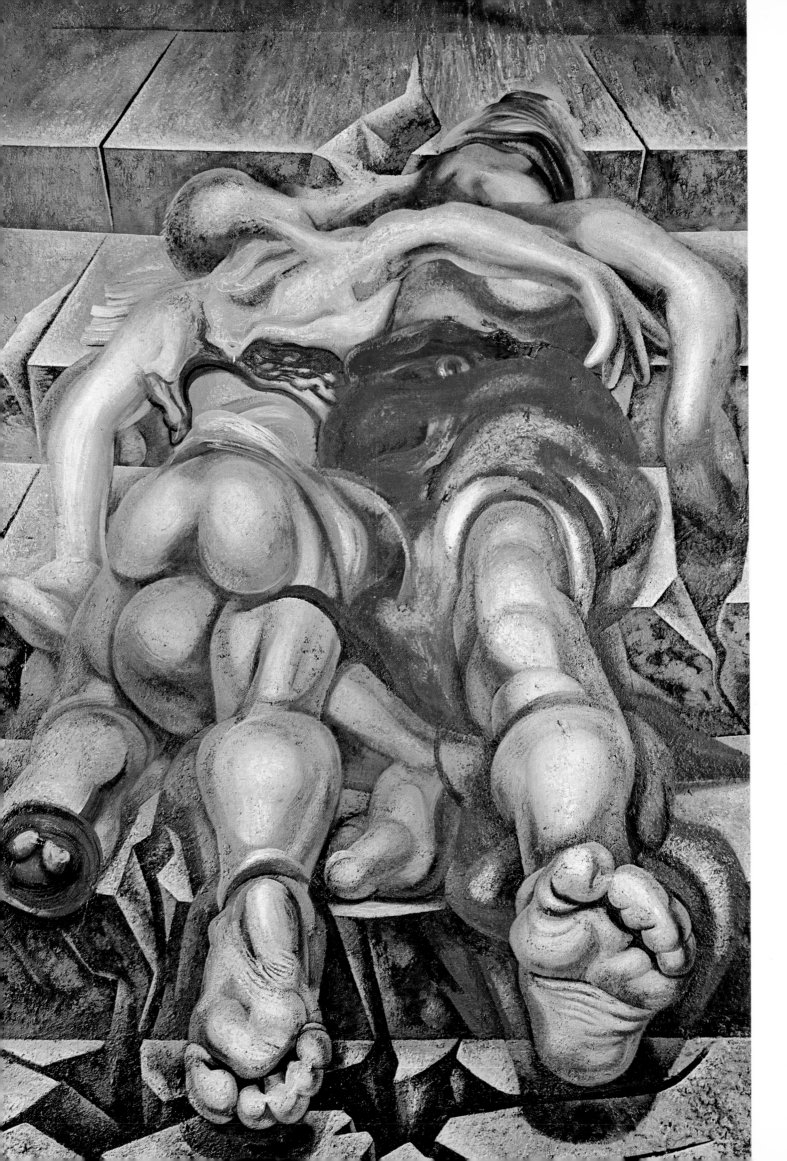

53

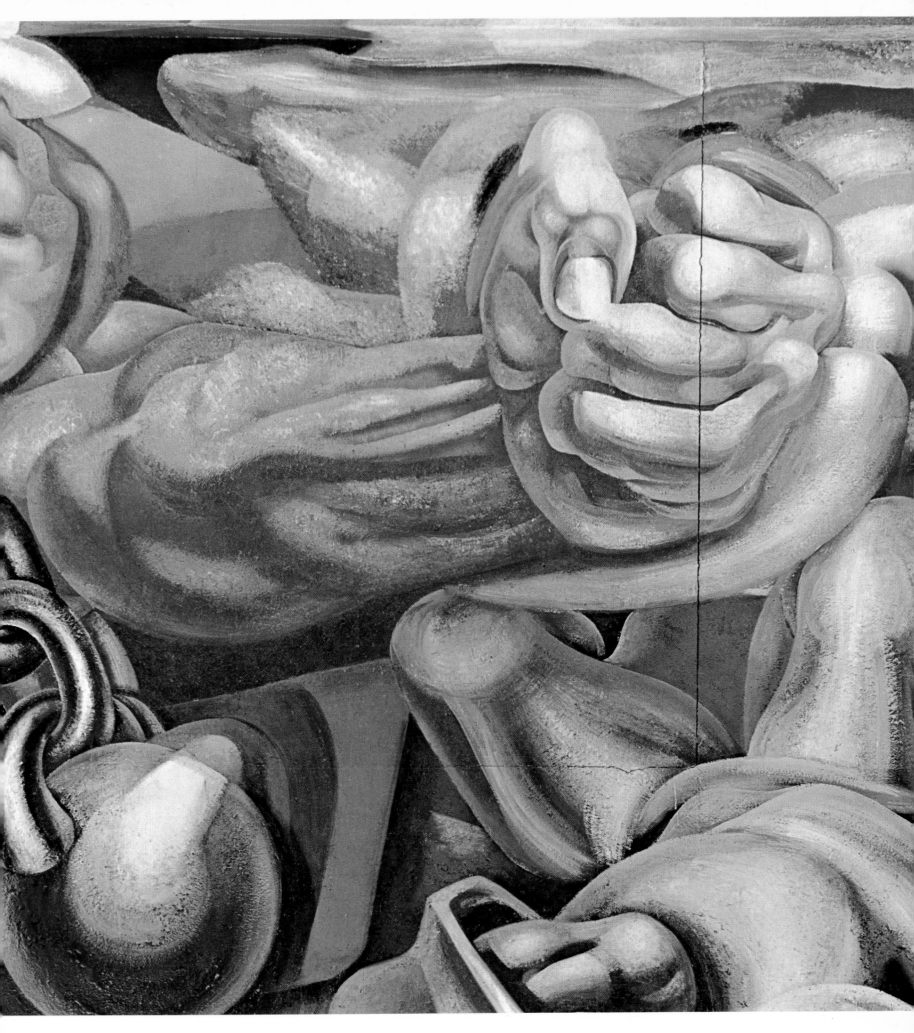

WORKS UP TO 1968

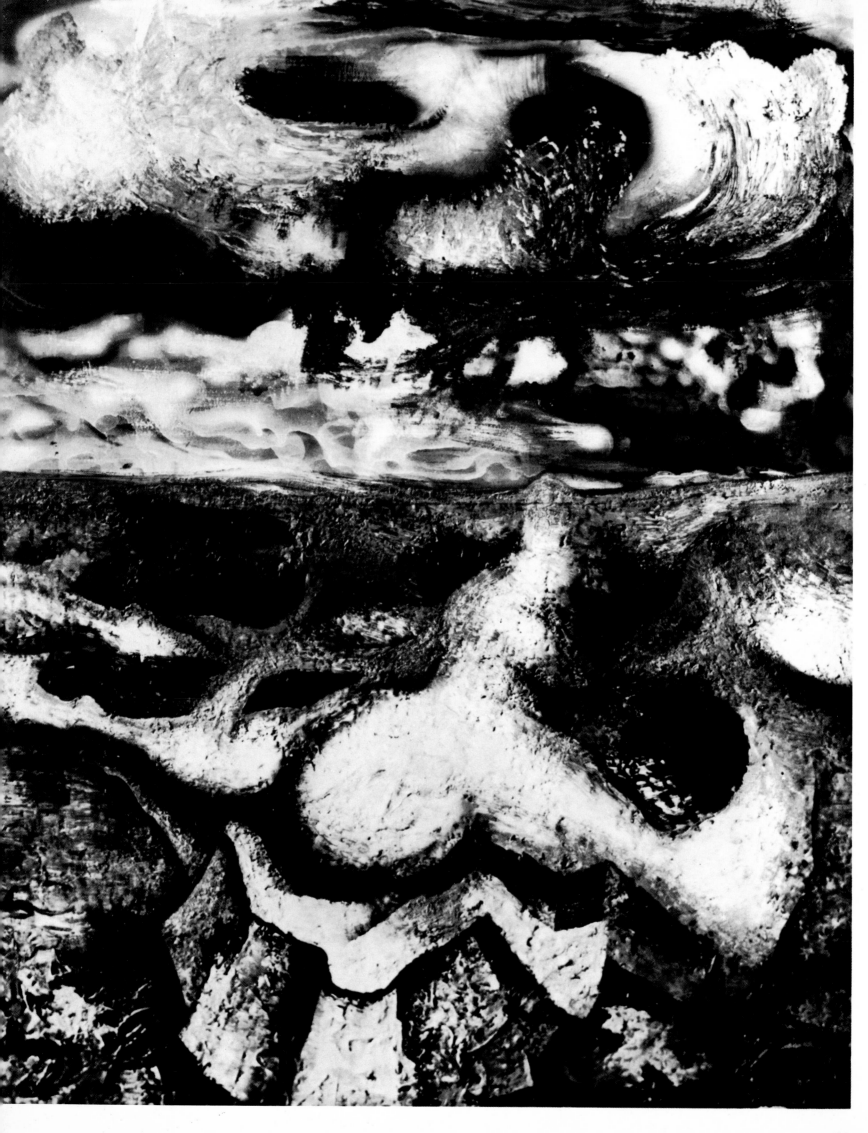

60

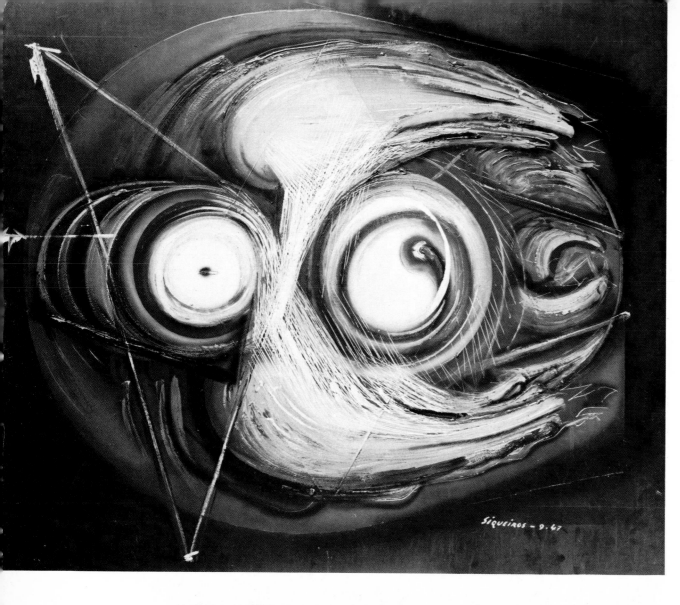

61

62

63

66

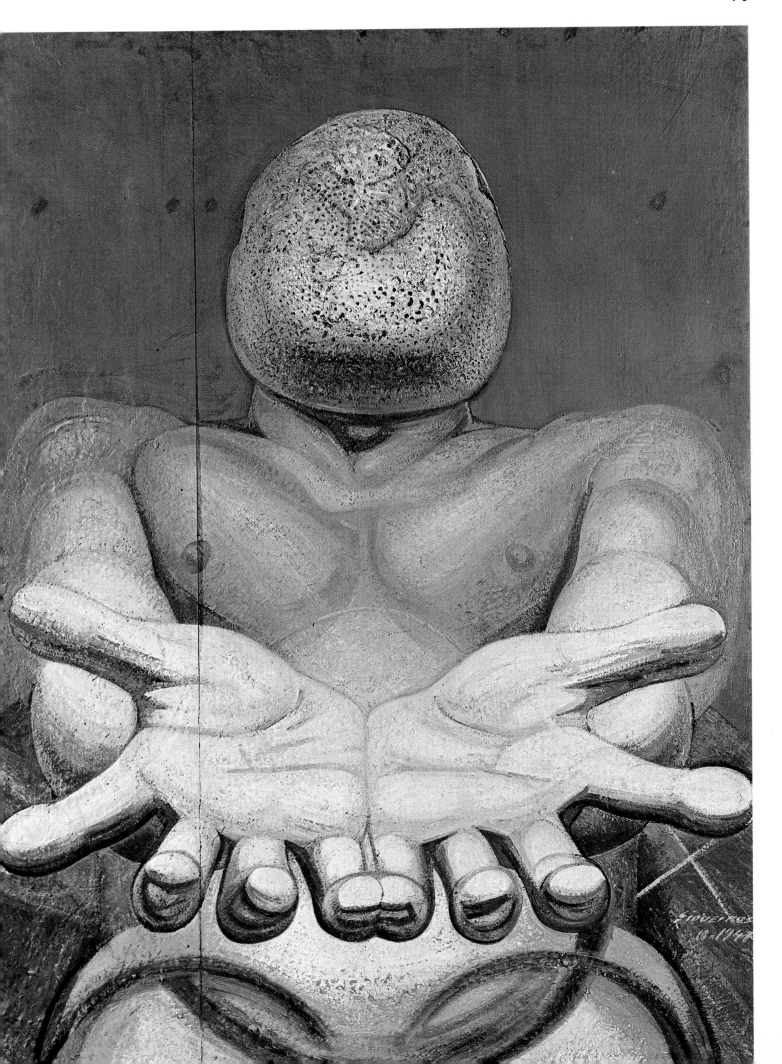

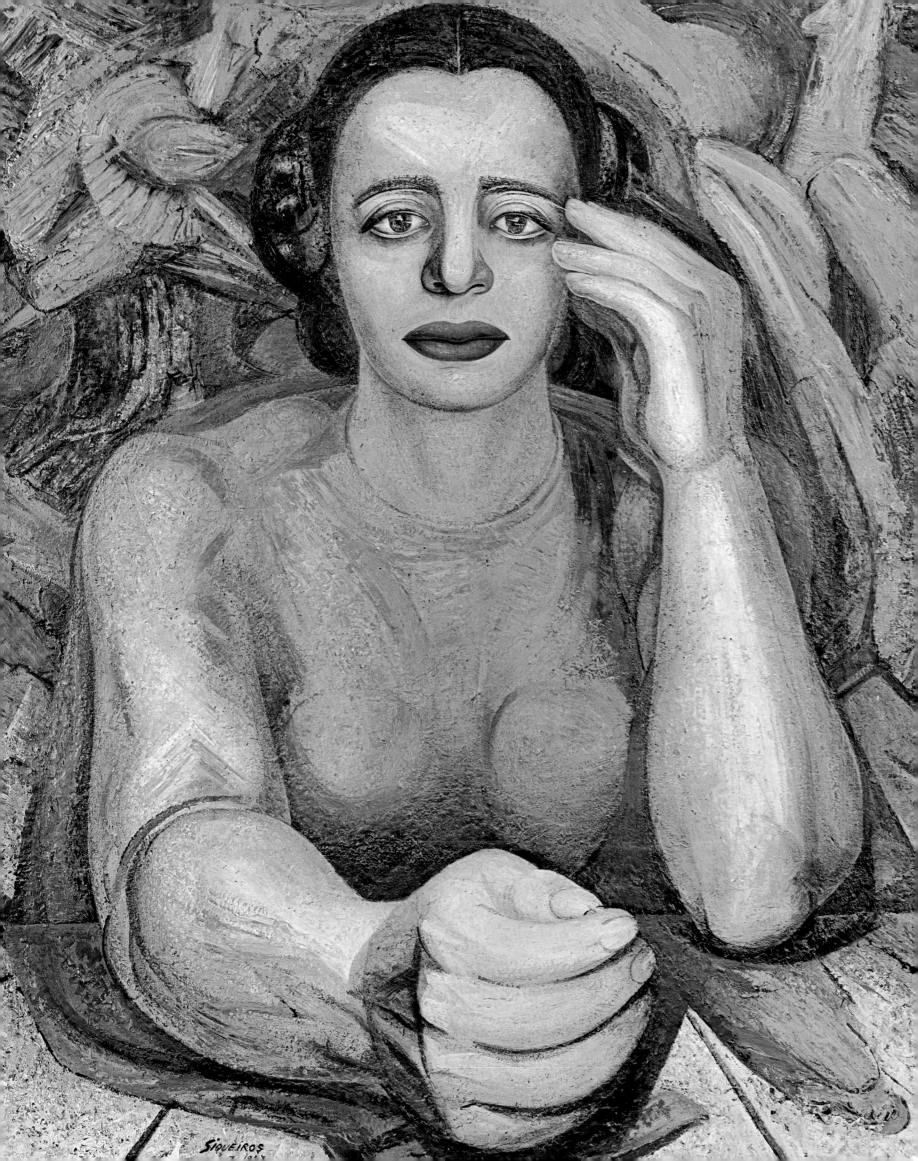

73

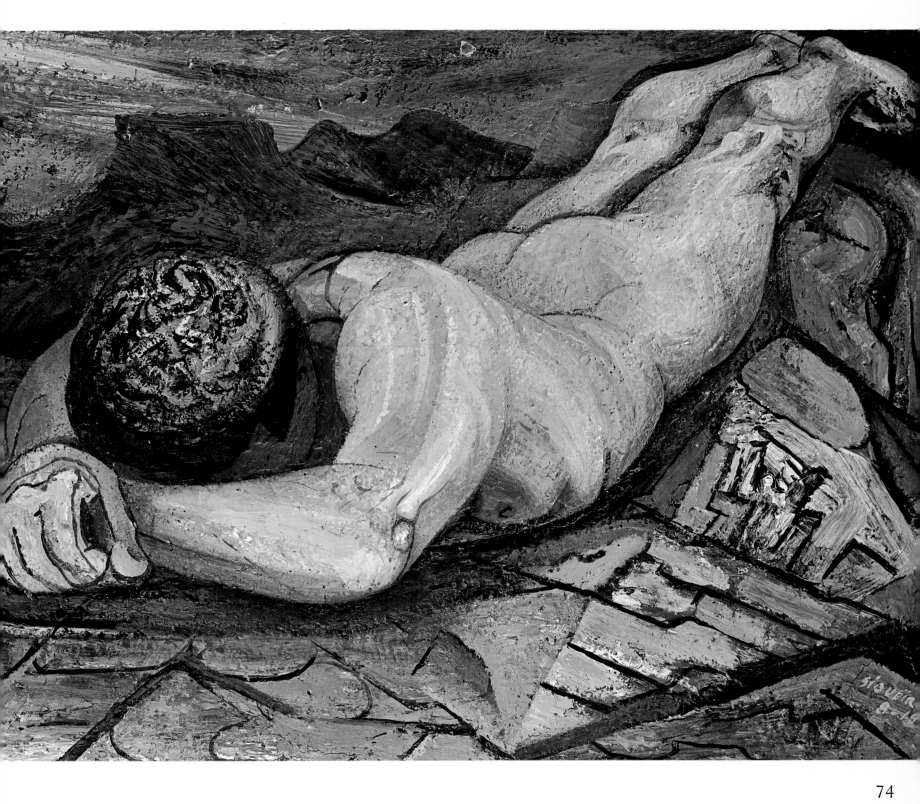

74

EXCOMUNION
Y
PENA DE MUERTE
PARA
MIGUEL HIDALGO
POR PROFESAR Y DIVULGAR
IDEAS EXOTICAS: PARTIDARIO
DE LA REVOLUCION DEMOCRATI-
CA FRANCESA.
POR DISOLUCION SOCIAL:
PRETENDE INDEPENDIZAR A
MEXICO DEL IMPERIO CO-
LONIAL ESPAÑOL. EN
CONSECUENCIA, POR
TRAIDOR A LA
PATRIA
30 DE JULIO
1811

Cuauhtémoc Reborn: Torture

mural 1951: (400 square feet)

82

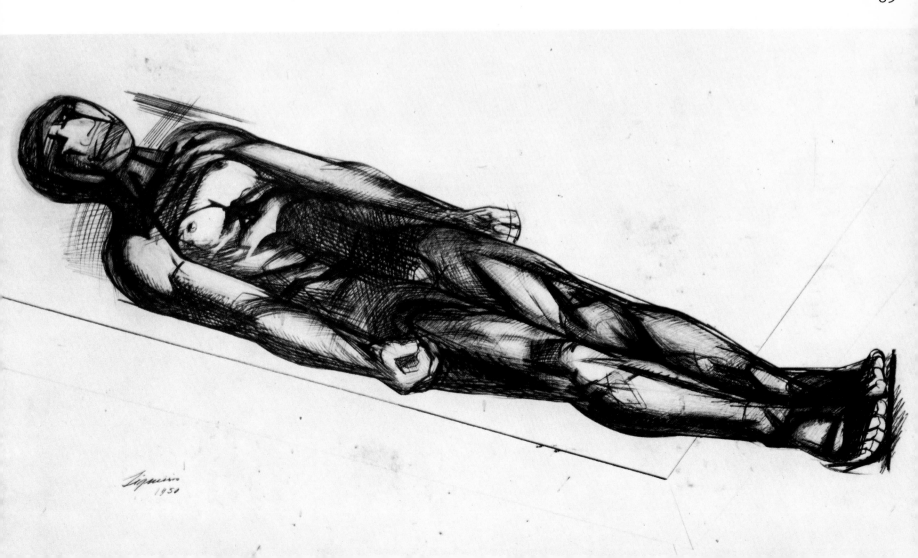

84

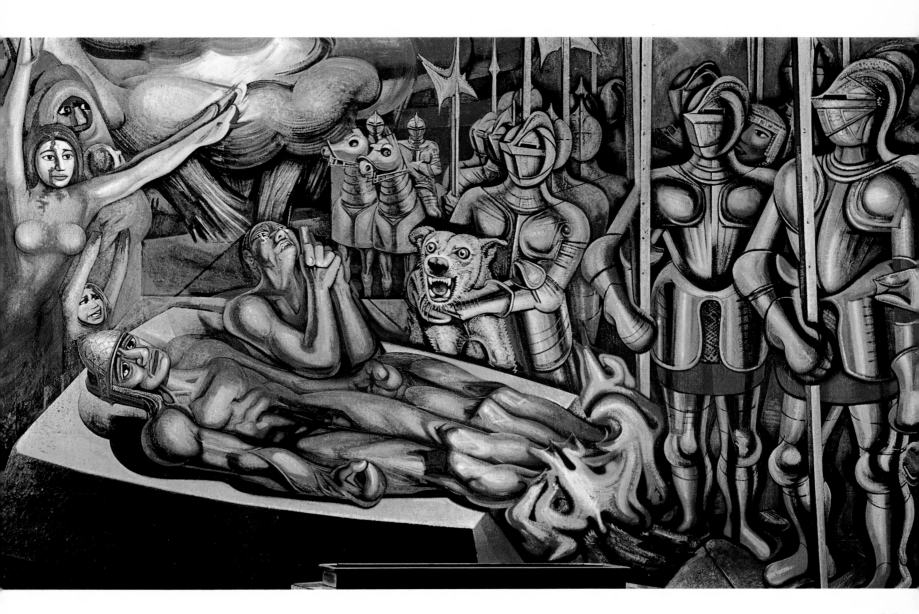

90

91

92 ▶

Cuauhtémoc Reborn: Resurrection

mural 1961: (400 square feet)

Patricians and Patricides

mural 1945–68:   (5,000 square feet)

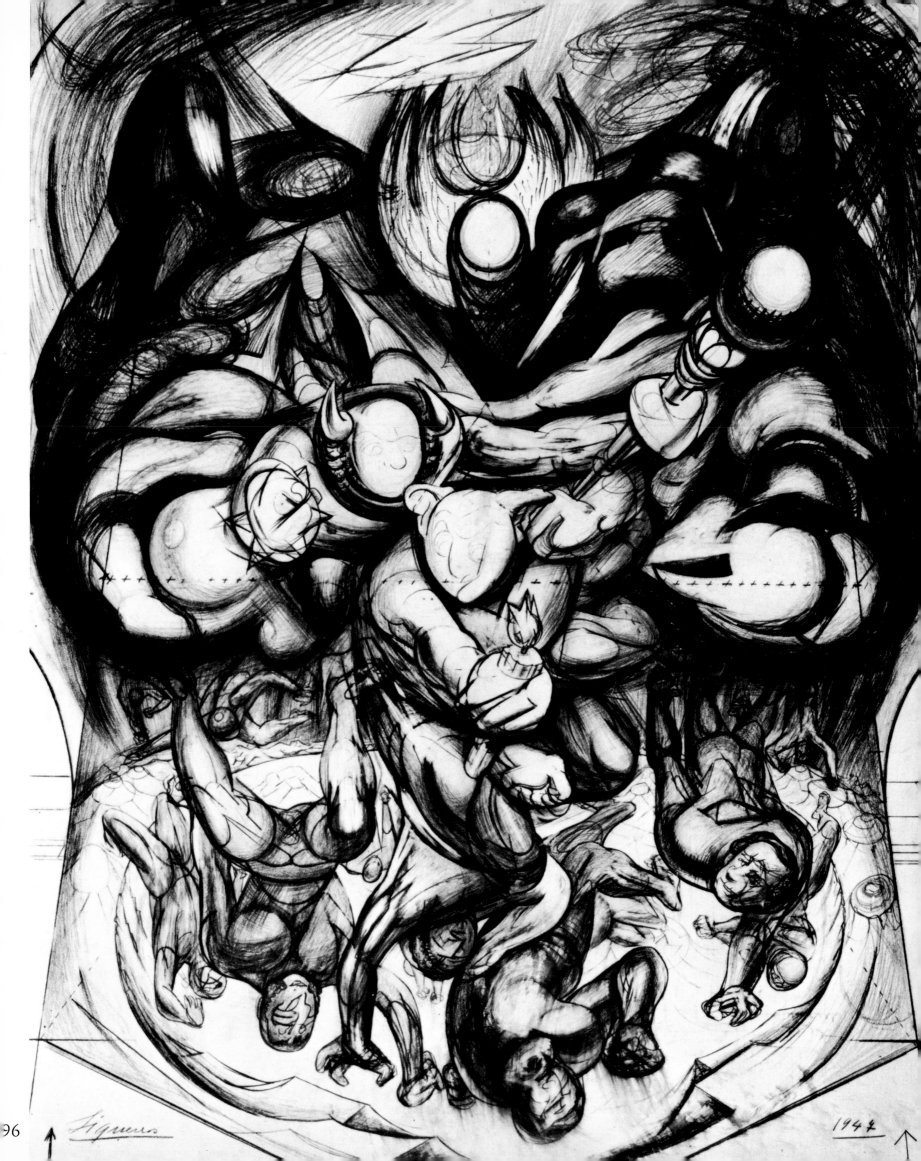

96

Siqueiros

1947

The People to the University, the University to the People

mural 1952–56:   (3,000 square feet)

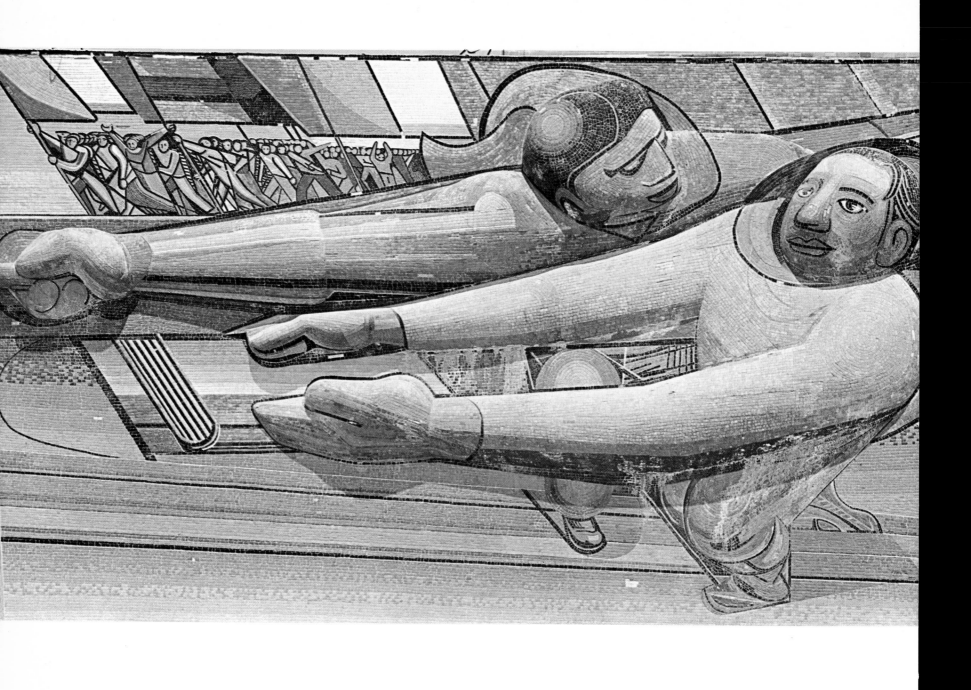

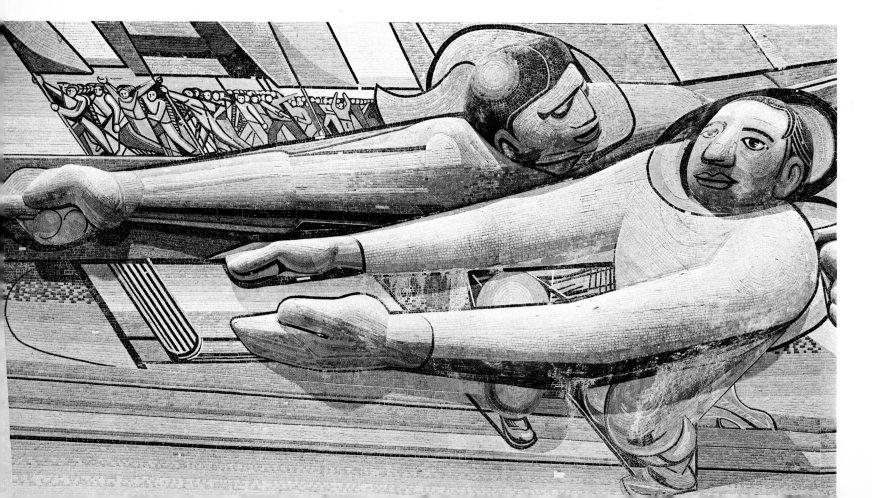

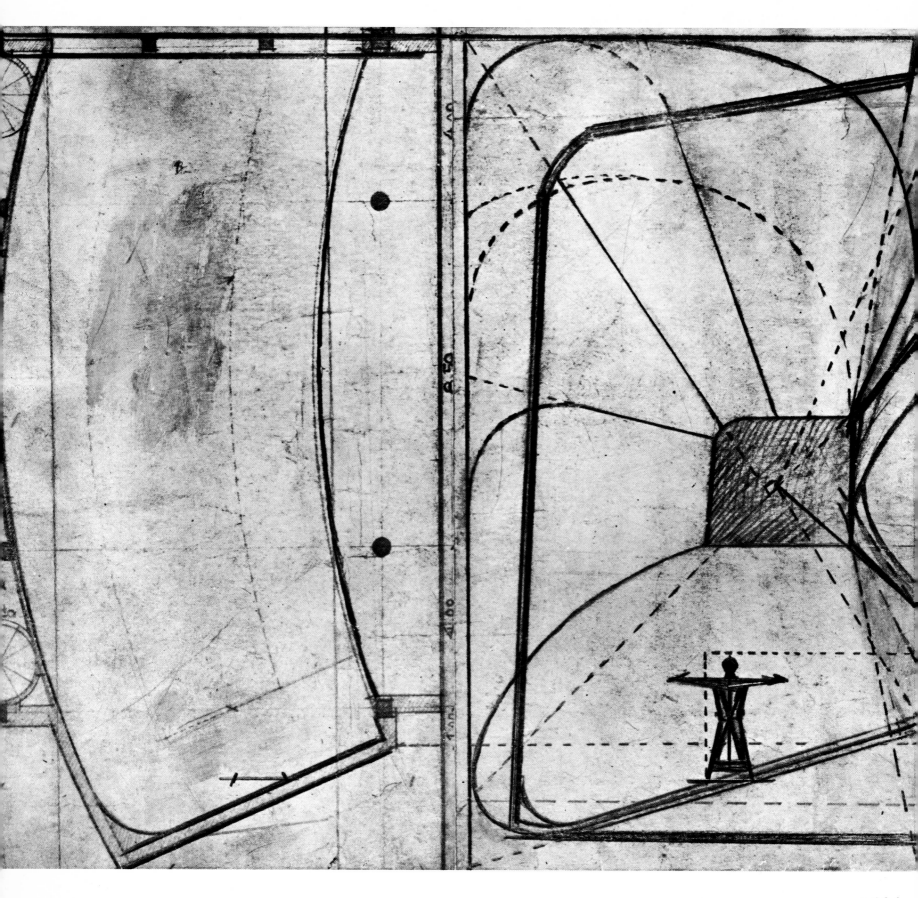

For the Complete Safety of All Mexicans at Work

mural 1952–54:   (3,000 square feet)

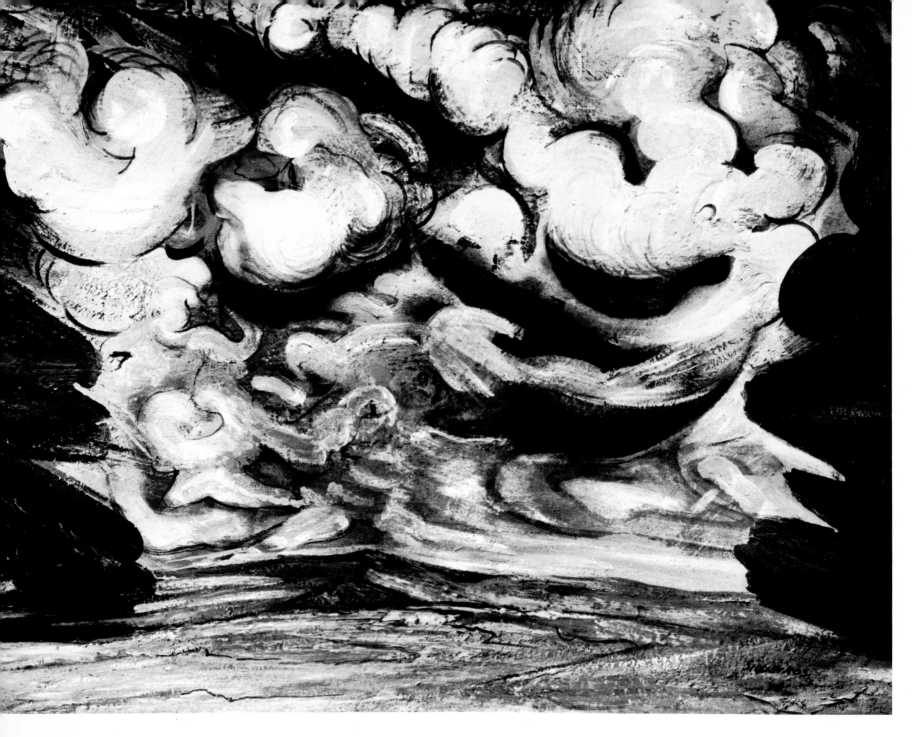

106

109

113

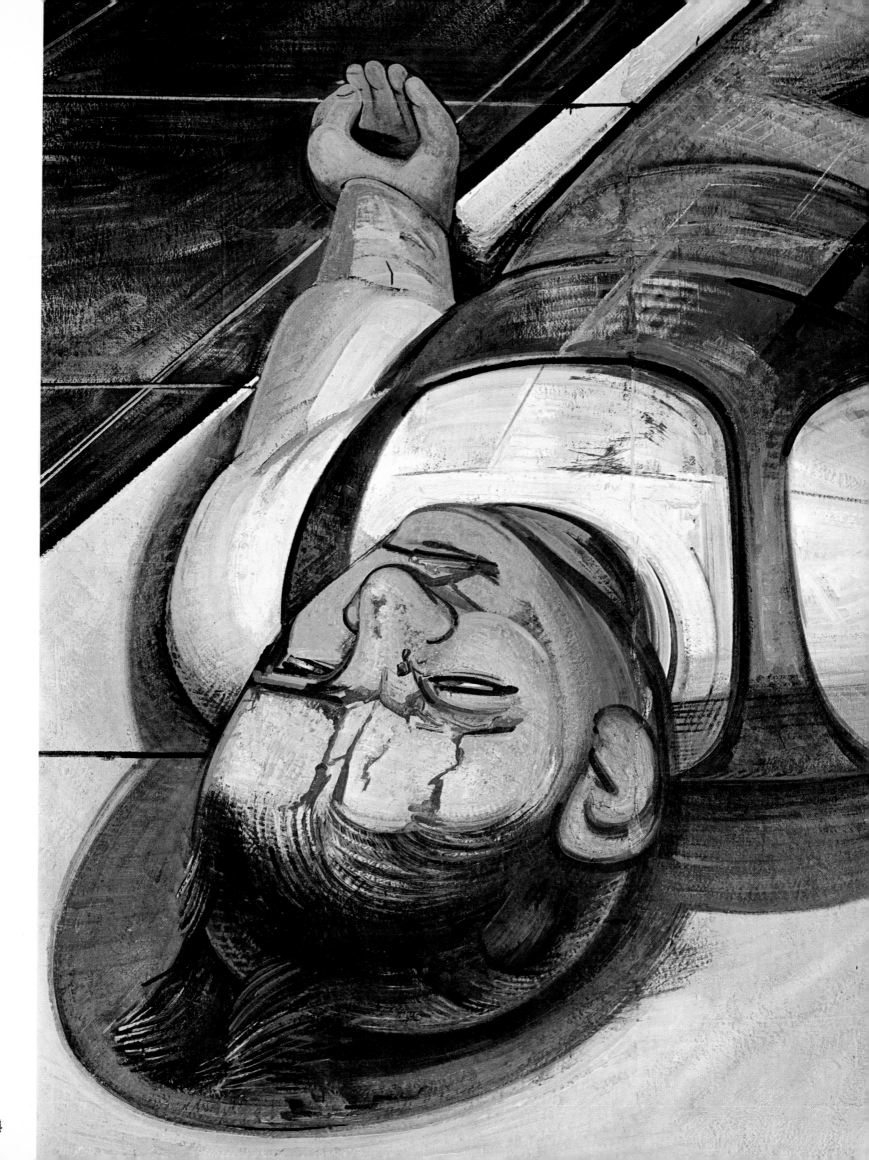

114

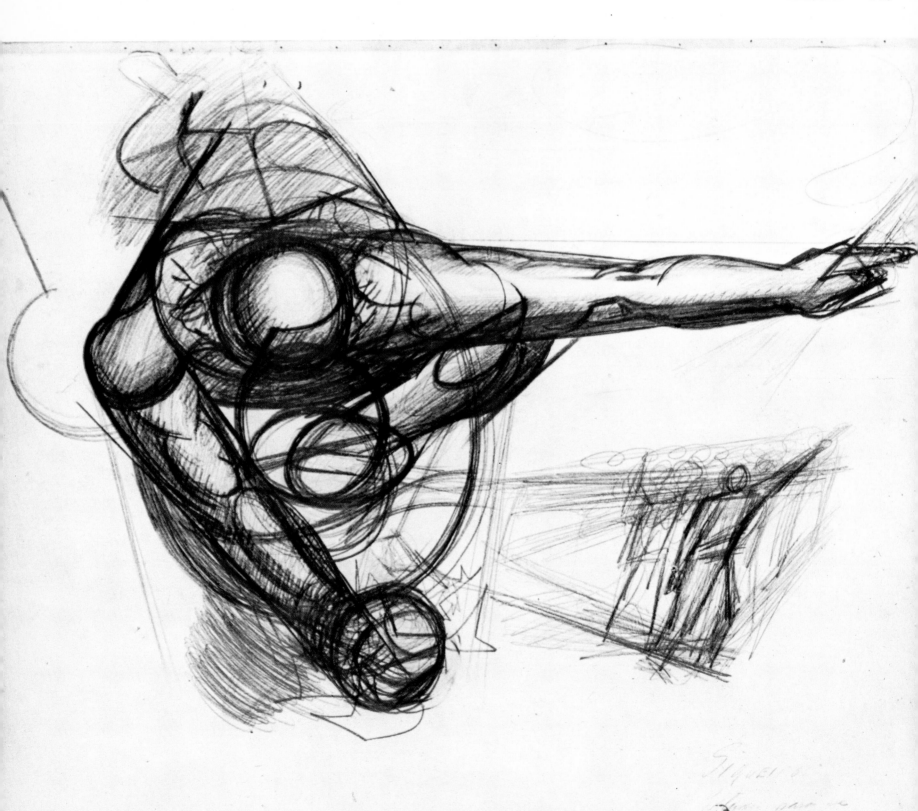

Apologia of the Future Victory of Medicine over Cancer

mural 1958

116

118

117

119

120

123

The Theater in Mexico

mural 1958: *(600 square feet)*

124

125

128

129

From Porfirio's Dictatorship to the Revolution

mural 1957–67: (about 4,500 square feet)

132

133

SIQUEIROS

137

138

139

143

March of Humanity in Latin America

mural 1964–68: (50,000 square feet)

144

145

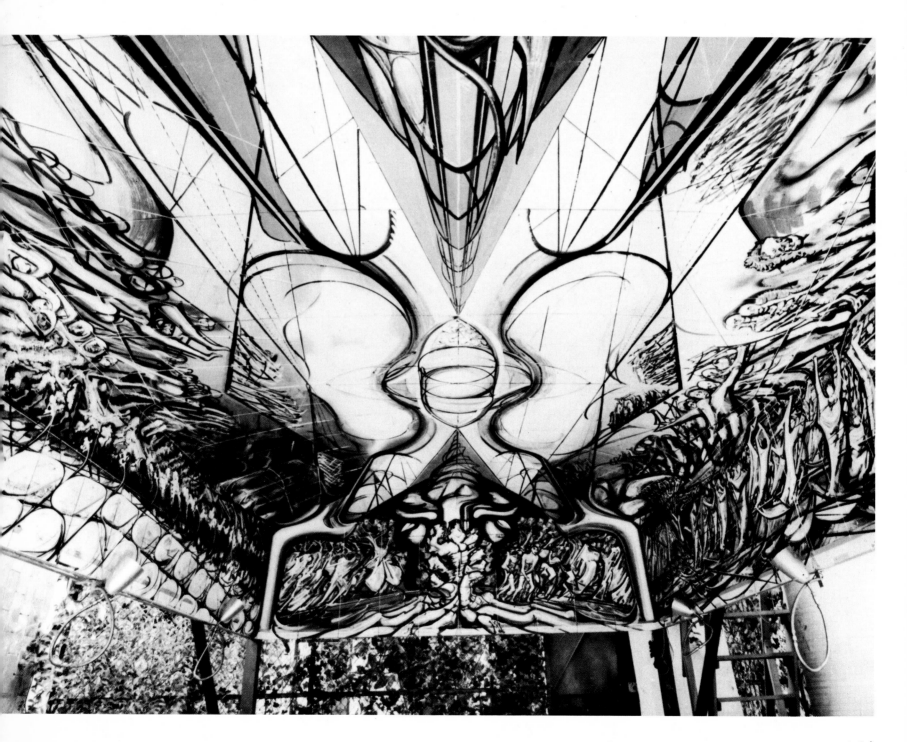

147

155

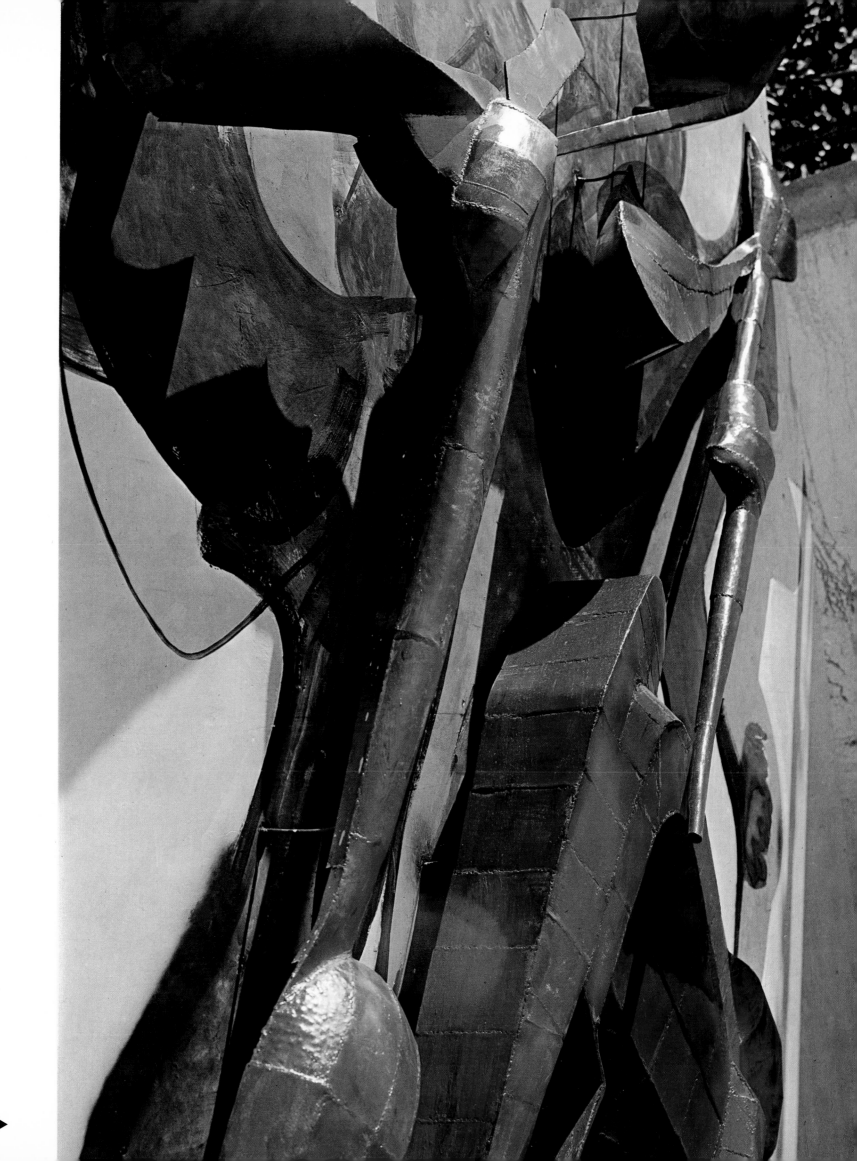